Dymphna Baird (nee Carvill) is originally from Northern Ireland. She left in the '70's to train as a primary school teacher in Newcastle upon Tyne. Throughout her teaching career, she has taught in South Ockendon, Essex; Waltham Cross, Hertforshire; Enfield Middlesex; and in an elementary school in Prince Rupert, British Columbia.

Dymphna is married with three sons and lives in Southgate, North London

To my family and wonderful friends who helped me survive
lockdown, especially Nancy and my Canadian Zoom
buddies.

Dymphna Baird

The Treasure of the Kingdom is Within

AUSTIN MACAULEY PUBLISHERS™

LONDON · CAMBRIDGE · NEW YORK · SHARJAH

A CIP catalogue record for this title is available from the British Library.

ISBN 9781787104846 (Paperback)
ISBN 9781786934123 (ePub e-book)

www.austinmacauley.com

First Published 2022
Austin Macauley Publishers Ltd®
1 Canada Square
Canary Wharf
London
E14 5AA

A huge thank you to Antoin Hanley, who not only proof read and encouraged me to publish "Pilgrimage to the Heart of God," but whose valuable insightful and hours spent proof reading and correcting the many errors, have allowed this book to be put forward for publication. His help and friendship have been greatly appreciated.

A huge thank you to Fr. Mehall Lowry and Fr. John Warnaby, who have, unknowingly, been my spiritual directors, while writing this book. Their spiritual insights and help were really appreciated.

To Mairead, Alison, Helen and Margaret who has been so helpful and encouraging in my writing career.

46524

"I shall give you a new heart, and put a new spirit within you" (Ezekiel 36:26).

God is love and has created us in love. The very essence of the Christian life is walking, growing, maturing, and developing in this love; so much easier to say than to do. No matter how well-meaning we start out somewhere, somehow we fall down, get a little complacent, or go wandering off in the wrong direction. That is why God, our Father, who created us, sent His son, Jesus to draw us back to Him, went even further and promised us that "I shall give you a new heart, and put a new spirit in you; I shall remove the heart of stone from your bodies and give you a heart of flesh instead. I shall put my Spirit in you and make you keep my laws and respect my observances." (Ezekiel 36:26–27)

Thus, we can rejoice because God is always faithful to his promises. He doesn't lead us down garden paths or put heavy burdens on us, demanding his pound of flesh. Instead, He created us in love and wants us to experience and grow in His unconditional love for us. So when Ezekiel prophesied that God would create "a new heart, and put a new spirit in you", and that he would, "remove the heart of stone from your bodies and give you a heart of flesh instead" (Ezekiel 36: 26), the message was loud and clear and it was that God wants to transform us, "(to) melt us, mould us, fashion us, into the image of Jesus His Son", according to the words of the hymn, Abba Father by Carey Landry, which was based on the metaphor from Isaiah. "And yet Yahweh, you are our Father; we the clay, you the potter, we are all the work of your hands" (Isaiah 64: 8–9).

Our God is a patient and careful Potter. He sees and loves us; our perfections, our imperfections; warts and all, even behind the mask we wear for others, and ourselves. Only too well does He know our blemishes, weaknesses, and the darkness within us; our many and varied sins. But that does not deter Him. He loves us so much that he wants to draw us into His glorious life. He wants to unite us with Him so deeply that every sin is wiped away, and every gift that he has given to us is developed to its fullest potential. It is for this reason He promised, "I will put a new Spirit within you" (Ezekiel 36:26). But not any spirit, His Spirit, the spirit of Jesus, the Holy Spirit.

In response to God's promise, all we have to do is humbly acknowledge our need of His Spirit; to desire His Spirit so we may become wise, sensible, sensitive people with devotion for all that is good, and just and truthful; for a new devotion to a loving father, through His most precious Son. This Spirit which we have been promised, is the great principle of light, life, and love, and this is the Spirit that God wants us to have. A new spirit to replace an arrogant, wilful, deceitful, spirit. Instead, we are promised one, which if allowed, will influence a new heart.

And so the promise continues, "I shall remove the heart of stone from your bodies and give you a heart of flesh." God wants to exchange our cold hardened hearts for a heart that is gentle, warm, soft, tender, and forgiving. A heart which is not cold, uncaring, hard, senseless, unfeeling, inflexible; but one which embraces love, cries out for love, can give, and receive love, unconditionally. One that is in tune with God, others and just as importantly, us. A heart of quite another temperament, assiduously listening to God's law, trembling at his closeness, moulded into willing compliance with his whole will; disposed to do, to be, or to suffer what God wills with faith, and in trust and hope. A heart that is open to listen to Him and to be obedient to His will; following the path of righteousness.

When we have accepted this new heart, God rejoices, and then comes the final part of the promise, "I will put *My* Spirit within you." Not just any spirit but God's spirit, an enlightening, regenerating, and sanctifying Spirit; that Holy Spirit which is given to and dwells in all true believers, all followers of Jesus; and allows us to powerfully, yet without compulsion, "keep (my) laws and respect my observances". Those commandments, the ones that Jesus summed up so beautifully when He said, "You must love the Lord your God with all your heart, with all your soul, and with all your mind. This is the greatest and the first commandment. The second resembles it: "You must love your neighbour as yourself. On these two commandments hang the whole law, and the Prophets also" (Matthew 34: 37-40). These laws or commandments exist for one purpose, they allow us to make informed choices, which bring us closer to the heart of God. We can choose to do right or wrong; to hurt or to reach out in love, to show compassion and empathy for four fellow men and women, or to ignore their plight and store up for ourselves all the riches this world has to offer. This choice is ours. If we desire God's Spirit, He will be true to his word and all we have to do is quite simply ask God to join His Spirit with our spirit.

Thus, by allowing our spirit to be renewed by God's Spirit, we respond to His call to holiness; a surrendering of our wills so we can readily comply with His will, in all things. We begin on the path to righteousness and holiness, living in obedience and love. That new beginning starts when we make a conscious decision to follow Christ and let Him be the Lord of our lives. When we surrender all to Him, He will fill us with His Spirit and it is this spirit living within us that will produce fruit, and just like any fruit-bearing plant, the evidence of the fruits comes after growth. And so it is with us; we won't see evidence of the Fruit of the Spirit in our lives the second we surrender our lives to Jesus. From a tiny seed, a tree will grow. Compacted into the seed are all the requirements needed for the plant to begin that growth and eventually produce fruit. For a tree to yield fruit, it goes through a cycle where it must be planted in good soil, nurtured with the right nutrients; watered and given a light source, until it reaches maturity. So it is with us in our Christian life.

In John's Gospel, Jesus used the metaphor of a plant, the vine, to explain the importance of our relationship with the Holy Trinity: God; the Father, God; the Son and God; the Holy Spirit, of how it is essential in leading a Christian life. "I am the true vine, and my father is the vine dresser" (15:1). The word 'true', is used here in the sense of real, being genuine. Jesus really and truly gives what is emblematically represented by a vine. All the nourishment of each branch and tendril which passes through the main stalk, or the vine, springs from the earth, or the word of God. Everyone that is a true follower of Jesus, who is united to Him by faith, will receive the benefits of His grace and His strength just, as the branch does from the vine. The word 'branch' includes all the boughs and the smallest tendrils that shoot out from the parent stalk. In this metaphor, Jesus is saying that he maintains the same relationship with his followers as the parent stalk does to the branches. We are joined to Him by believing in him; surrendering our dependence to him; accepting our need of him; but most of all of us embracing him as our Saviour, Redeemer, and Friend. Our attachment forms a bond and thus, we become united to him where we seek the same objectives; are willing to encounter the same trials, contempt, persecution, to the point where we are desirous that his Father shall be our Father – His home, our home.

It is a union of friendship, love, and dependence, even interdependence. After all, if a branch is withered, it will not produce fruit. "Anyone who does not remain in me is like a branch that has been thrown away – he withers" (John 15:6), and then Jesus went on to explain, "It is to the glory of my father that you should bear much fruit." It is a two-way situation, as the Father is dependent on us to make others aware of the external manifestation of His being. Thus this joining together, a union of weakness with strength; of imperfection with perfection; a dying of self to unite our spirit with a living Saviour; of a lost sinner with an unchanging Friend and Redeemer, has the power to change the lives of, not only ourselves but all those around us.

However, this union benefits us the most. Once we have become united to Him, we will be well looked after. "And my father is the vinedresser. Every branch in me that bears no fruit he cuts away, and every branch that bears fruit he prunes

13

to make it bear even more" (John 15: 2-3). The two chief duties of the vinedresser are to cut off all fruitless tendrils and cleansing those that bear fruit gives an illustration of a very hands-on Father, tending to the basic needs which will allow growth and maturity to occur producing an intended outcome for all His children who are followers of Jesus His son. It is the relationship between a shepherd and his sheep, that of loving nourishing, caring, tending, relationship.

Just as a shepherd lovingly tends to the needs of his sheep, so too does the gardener tend to his plants. He will prune away all that is preventing the plan's growth. By removing all dead parts, the plant begins to thrive again and grows into maturity. In the same way, God purifies all true Christians, so that they may become more useful if they but allow His Spirit to work within them. He will take away all that which hinders our usefulness. He will nourish us, revive us, and make us aware of our motives, which influence our actions within our everyday life. This he does by the regular influences of his Spirit in sanctifying us, purifying our motives, teaching us the beauty of holiness, and inducing us to devote ourselves more to him. He does it by taking away what opposes our usefulness, however much we may be attached to it, or however painful it may be to part with it; as a vinedresser will often feel himself compelled to lop off a branch that is large, apparently thrifty, and handsome, but which bears no fruit, and which shades or injures those which do. So God will remove the objects which bind our affections, our worthless idols, to allow us to grow and flourish.

If a plant is not growing, it's dying, and so it is with us. In our spiritual life, we need to be quietly, gently growing because if we are not then we too can be dying. Without constant supervision disease, lack of water and light, overbearing trees, and encroachment of weeds can lead to non-productivity, and eventual death with a plant; and likewise with our spiritual life, if we try to lead a life without the Holy Spirit. Paul, when writing to the Galatians, explained the dangers of not living a spirit-filled life. "Let me put it like this; if you are guided by the Spirit you will be in no danger of yielding to self-indulgence since self-indulgence is the opposite of the Spirit, the Spirit is totally against such a thing, and it is precisely because the two are so opposed that you do not always carry out your good intentions. When self-indulgence is at work the results are obvious, fornication, gross indecency, sexual irresponsibility; idolatry and sorcery; feuds, wrangling, jealousy, bad temper, quarrels, disagreements, factions, envy drunkenness, orgies and similar things" (Galatians 5: 5-20). He warned, "Those that behave like this will not inherit the kingdom of God" (5:22). We can't belong to a spiritual kingdom and an earthly kingdom. "No one can be a slave of two masters; he will either hate the first and love the second or treat the first with respect and the second with scorn. You cannot be the slave of both God and money" (Matthew 6:24). Although money is used in this instance, there are many other selfish pleasures we indulge in which could be used instead of the word, 'money'. Indeed, whatever we are willing to invest time, strength, passion into accumulating, appeasing, and which will allow us to increase our pleasures, our earthly treasures, those which we will have to leave when we die, all of these could be used instead of 'money', as these are our idols.

After the warning about living an earthly life, Paul continues his letter in a more positive vein. The negativity that was displayed in the first part of chapter 5 is vastly contrasted in the latter part. In this chapter, Paul sets out clear objectives on how we can inherit the kingdom, the virtues we need to develop, and just as Jesus had used the metaphor of the vine, Paul also used a metaphor, this time it was the product of a healthy plant. He uses nine visible attributes of a true Christian spiritual life. "What the Spirit brings is very different: love, joy, peace, patience, kindness, goodness, faithfulness (trustfulness) gentleness and self-control" (Galatian 5:22–23).

Consequently, these nine visible attributes of the true Christian life, have become known as the Fruits of the Spirit. They are a physical manifestation of a Christian's transformed life. Although there are nine, they are all intertwined, bound together, like the branches of a vine. Even if we would like to think of them as such, they are not individual 'fruits'. So, unfortunately, we can't pick and choose which ones we want to develop. Rather, the fruit of the Spirit is an amalgamated 'fruit' that is characterized by all who truly walk in the Holy Spirit. As Christians, we need to be producing and displaying these fruits in our new lives, in our daily walk with each other, after all, we are the only face of Jesus others may see.

Quite simply, the only way to produce the Fruit of the Spirit is to have the Holy Spirit living, active, within us. This initial step happens when we believe, "Blessed be God, the Father of our Lord Jesus Christ, who has blessed us with all spiritual blessing of heaven in Christ. Before the world was made, he chose us, chose us in Christ, to be holy and spotless, and to live through love in his presence, determining that we should become his adopted sons, through Jesus Christ for his own kind purposes, to make us praise the glory of his grace, his free gift to us of his beloved, in whom through his blood we gain our freedom, the forgiveness of our sins" (Ephesians 1:3-8). "Now you too in him, have heard the message of the truth and the good news of your salvation, and have believed it." And thus because we have heard and believed we "too have been stamped with the seal of the Holy Spirit of the promise, the pledge of our inheritance which brings freedom for those whom God has taken for his own, to make his glory praised" (Ephesians 1:13–14), when we allow Him to rule in our hearts.

At the beginning of His earthly ministry, Jesus preached that "the kingdom of God is close at hand" (Matthew 4:17). In Jesus' teaching, the kingdom of God was to be a central theme. God is king, and his rule was now being made effective. In Luke's Gospel, the Kingdom of God is also mentioned. When the disciples were being sent out, they were given the instruction, "Whenever you go into a town where they make you welcome, eat what is set before you. Cure those in it who are sick, and say, 'The kingdom of God is very near to you'" (Luke 10:9). Their message was to be that the kingdom of God had arrived; the signs of its presence were the mighty works which they would perform. Thus when the gospel is proclaimed, the blessings connected with God's rule, His kingdom, are near or within the grasp of all who will accept them.

This theme also appeared in Mark's gospel. "Now after John was arrested, Jesus came into Galilee, proclaiming the gospel of God, and saying, "The time is fulfilled, and the kingdom of God is at hand; repent and believe in the gospel" (Mark 1:14–15). This was the beginning; the rule of God was about to begin on earth. The kingdom of God was shown first in the life of Jesus, and then in the lives of his followers. The word *gospel* simply means 'good news', and the term 'kingdom' comes from the Greek word *basileia*, which means 'the realm in which a sovereign king rules'. Throughout the New Testament, the word *kingdom* occurs one hundred and sixty-two times and depending on the context, the meaning is often open to debate. However there is a common consensus that the kingdom consistently refers to the rule of Christ in the hearts of believers when we allow our hearts to be moulded like His, and we receive His Spirit within us. "Because the kingdom of God does not mean eating or drinking this or that, it means righteousness and peace and joy brought by the Holy Spirit" (Romans 14:17).

Paul finished his letter to the Romans with a blessing, incorporating the second and third fruit of the Spirit, with the seventh, "May the God of hope bring you such joy and peace in your faith that the power of the Holy Spirit will remove all bounds to hope" (Romans 15:13).

It is this same Spirit, God's Spirit that Ezekiel prophesied, and Paul spoke about. The Spirit which God would put within us. If we willingly accept His Spirit, He will rule in our hearts, transforming, renewing, and nourishing us: allowing us to blossom in love. Not only that but we will be filled with joy! The joy which Paul talked about in Romans (14:17) is so often overlooked but is an integral part of the Christian life.

Chapter One
Joy

"For you shall go out in joy and be led forth in peace; the mountains and the hills before you shall break forth into singing, and all the trees of the field shall clap their hands" Isaiah (55:12).

"Joy is the flag flown high from the banner of my heart for the King is in residence there" (Joy Is the Flag – by writer unknown – is a children's hymn). It is normally sung with great gusto and indeed who can watch an Olympic parade, without witnessing the joy of the flag bearer as they walk, or in some cases try to dance, into the arena, waving their country's flag with all their might.

When googling the word, 'joy', the definition given is a feeling of great pleasure and happiness, with associated synonyms which include: pleasure, joyfulness, jubilation, triumph, exultation, rejoicing all of which are normally associated within a spiritual context.

However, the list also contains emotions such as; happiness, gladness, glee, exhilaration, ebullience, exuberance, elation, euphoria, bliss, ecstasy, transports of delight, rapture, and radiance, so although similar in meaning they are distinguished by having different depths to the emotion. According to the 'The Theology of Joy-George Thomas.docx', there are fifteen different Hebrew words and eight Greek words to describe 'joy', all of them having interchangeable uses, sometimes joy being used as a noun while at other times as a verb. Depending on the usage, joy can be an emotion; a source or cause of keen pleasure or delight; an expression or display of glad feelings or festive gaiety and a state of extreme happiness. Therefore, although joy as an emotion is intangible, it can be made tangible through our actions, of happiness and love.

Indeed, when watching the flagbearer, it is clear to observe their almost tangible joy. Their happiness, or joy, is like a smile, it is infectious. This inner emotion of joy is manifested in outward rejoicing, exhilaration, exuberance, and triumph: And why not? Whether they win a medal or not, they have triumphed, having reached the pinnacle of their career. Their achievements have been recognised and consequently, they had been given the highest sporting accolade awarded to a sportsperson, that of being chosen by their country to represent them. All the hard work, the long gruelling hours, the monotonous, limited diet have not been in vain. Thus joy, in this special moment didn't just happen but was an accumulation of various elements, a process involving possibly hardships even suffering to overcome frailties. They had chosen to strive (in the name of the legacy of the London 2012 Olympics), 'to be the best we (they) can be'. Joy was their inward reward, not something they would have set out to achieve as joy is an emotion, a spontaneous reaction which we have no immediate control over. No matter what their circumstances, at that present moment in time, for those flagbearers, their happiness was clear for all to see.

Joy is synonymous with happiness. However, there are subtle differences. Joy springs from within and is an internal experience. Happiness is caused by external circumstances or experiences. Both do, however, involve pleasurable feelings and both are mentioned in the New and Old Testament, happy or happiness thirty times (depending on the Bible version) while joy or rejoice appears over three hundred times.

In the Old Testament, joy covers a wide range of human and spiritual experiences, all involving causes for real celebration, from nature to victory in battle and more importantly, the return of exiles. Indeed the spiritual joys are often expressed by the metaphors of feasting, marriage, and victory in battle. Psalm 126 (5-6,) for example, refers to a plentiful harvest but is also used to describe the believer's final victory over his adversaries:

> May those who sow in tears
> reap with shouts of joy!
> He that goes forth weeping
> bearing the seed for sowing
> shall come home with shouts of joy,
> bringing his sheaves with him. (Psalm 126:5-6)

This theme of a loving, merciful God who gives victory to his people and causes 'joy', is also found in other psalms, but is more specifically related to the return of exiles:

"May we shout with joy for your victory, and plant our banners in the name of the Lord" (Psalm 20:5).

In the ballad of the exiles, Psalm 137, there is anticipated joy for the exiles' return, "May I never speak again, if I forget You!

If I do not count Jerusalem

The greatest of my joys".

While in Exodus we learn that "Jethro rejoiced at all Yahweh's goodness to Israel in rescuing them from Egyptian's hands" (Exodus 18:9-11).

Joy is also referred to Israel's return from the Babylonian exile,

"Shout with joy for Jacob! Hail the chief of the nations! Proclaim! Praise! Shout:

Yahweh has saved his people, the remnant of Israel" (Jer.31:7-8).

Throughout the Old Testament there are numerous references to joy, springing from the Spiritual life, in knowing and serving God:

"The hope of the righteous brings joy, but the expectation of the wicked will perish" (Proverbs, 10: 28).

"The LORD is my strength and my shield; in him my heart trusts, and I am helped; my heart exults, and with my song, I give thanks to him" (Psalm 28:7).

"The precepts of the LORD are right, rejoicing the heart; the commandment of the LORD is pure, enlightening the eyes" (Psalm 19:8).

Our soul awaits Yahweh, he is our help and our shield; our hearts rejoice in him, we trust in his holy name" (Psalm 33:20).

Wine was often used in the Old Testament to represent joy, both in celebration, and festivity, expressing the abundant blessings of God. In the ancient Near East, with its scarcity of water, wine was a necessity rather than a luxury, so it came to symbolize sustenance and life. "Then he said to them, 'Go your way. Eat the fat and drink sweet wine and send portions to anyone who has nothing ready, for this day is holy to our Lord. And do not be grieved, for the joy of the LORD is your strength'" (Nehemiah 8:10).

Not only is joy encountered in the spiritual life but is often referred to in worship in the Old Testament; indeed it is regarded as an integral part of worship:

"Then I will go to the altar of God, To God my exceeding joy; And upon the lyre, I shall praise You, O God, my God." (Psalm 43:4)

The Psalmist even instructs us to incorporate joy into our worship; "Shout joyfully to the Lord, all the earth; Break forth and sing for joy and sing praises" (Psalm 98:4-6) because "The Lord is my strength and my shield; My heart trusts in Him, and I am helped; Therefore my heart exults, And with my song, I shall thank Him (Psalm 28:7). My lips will shout for joy when I sing praises to You; And my soul, which You have redeemed (Psalm 71:23). O come, let us sing for joy to the Lord, Let us shout joyfully to the rock of our salvation" (Psalm 95:1).

It is not only the abundance of the harvest but also childbirth which can be a cause of great joy but also can be used metaphorically: "He gives the barren woman a home, making her the joyous mother of children" (Psalm 113:9, NEV). The barren woman, in this case, a completely hopeless and irreversible situation being reversed into that of hope and a cause of celebration due to the intervention of a loving merciful God.

There are similar causes of joy; birth; delight in the Lord, help from the Lord; victory over death; found in the New Testament. However, in the New Testament generally, joy and gladness, rejoicing and celebration quite often are connected with Jesus; his disciples; the birth of the church; and the lives of early Christians. In contrast to Mark and Matthew's gospel, which have few references to joy and rejoicing, Luke's gospel has not only the most references but also the most detailed prescription for joy. It can't be coincidental that Luke's gospel contains also the in-depth story of the birth of Jesus, a cause for all Christians to feel great joy and jubilation.

Luke's Gospel begins with the joy associated with birth and in particular a special birth, that of John the Baptist. "The angel said to Zechariah: 'Your wife Elizabeth is to bear you a son, and you must name him John. He will be your joy and delight, and many will rejoice at his birth, for he will be great in the sight of the Lord'" (Luke 1:13-15). The angel foretold Zechariah that John would be not only his joy but also that many would rejoice at his birth. "Meanwhile the time came for Elizabeth to have her child, and she gave birth to a son; and when her neighbours and relations heard that the Lord had shown her so great a kindness, they shared her joy" (Luke 1: 57–58). This joy shared between Elizabeth, her family, and neighbours, was much more than that caused by the birth of a child, to a woman considered barren. The fact that she had conceived was attributed to the loving mercy of God. People in ancient Israel believed that a large family was a blessing from God. Infertility, therefore, was a source of humiliation and shame. Indeed, there was a widely held belief that if a Jewish woman remained childless, it was because of the woman's sinfulness. Therefore the birth of a child to someone who was considered to be barren was seen as a sign that not only was the woman blessed but more importantly a great blessing would come to the people through the child, especially notable are Isaac the son of Abraham and Sarah, Samuel the son of Elkanah and his first wife Hanna, (1 Samuel 1:1–2:21) and Samson the son of Manoah (Judges 13:1–4). Not only were these sons born from mothers who were considered barren, but they also went on to do great things for the Jewish nation.

Indeed, Samson's birth had similar parallels to that of the announcement of the birth of Jesus, to Mary. However, when the angel announced the forthcoming birth, there was no mention of the word 'rejoice' or 'joy'. We are told in Judges that 'an angel of Yahweh' appeared to Samson's mother, the wife of Manoah, who belonged to the tribe of Dan (Judges 13:3). "The angel of the LORD appeared to her and said, 'You are barren and childless, but you are going to become pregnant and give birth to a son.'" After she was told that she would have a child, she went and told her husband, "A man of God has just come to me. His presence was like the presence of an angel of God, he was so majestic. I didn't ask him where he came from, and he didn't tell me his name. But he said to me, 'You will become pregnant and have a son. Now then, drink no wine or other fermented drink and do not eat anything unclean, because the boy will be a Nazirite of God from the womb until the day of his death'" (Judges 13:67).

Although no angel appeared to Samuel's mother, Hannah, she, like Samson's mother, was also barren but her pain was compounded by her husband's other wife who not only bore children but taunted Hannah mercilessly. Every year, Elkanah, Hannah's husband, would offer a sacrifice at the Shiloh sanctuary, and give Peninnah, his second wife and her children a portion but he gave Hannah a double portion "because he loved her, and the LORD had closed her womb" (1 Samuel 1:5, NIV). One day, while Hannah was in the temple, she prayed with great weeping (I Samuel 1:10), while Eli, the High Priest, was sitting on a chair near the doorpost. In her prayer, she asked God for a son and in return, she vowed to give the son back to God so that he could serve Him. After Hannah and her husband, Elkanah, returned from Shiloh to their home at Ramah, they slept together. Scripture says, "…and the Lord remembered her" (1 Samuel 1:19, NIV). She became pregnant, had a son, and named him Samuel, which means 'God hears'.

Names play an important part in the birth stories. "In the sixth month, the angel, Gabriel, was sent by God to a town in Galilee called Nazareth, to a virgin betrothed to a man named Joseph, of the house of David; and the virgin's name was Mary." Unlike the announcement of the angel to Samson's mother, this time, the angel is named. Only the angels. Gabriel and Raphael. are named in the bible so when mention is made of 'an angel of the Lord', it is assumed that it is not Gabriel or Raphael. The name Gabriel means, 'God is great', and, it is Gabriel who revealed the names of both John, (which means God is gracious) and Jesus, in the announcement of their birth. Not only was Mary told to call the child Jesus, but Joseph also received the same instruction, in a dream, when an angel of the Lord appeared to him, "You shall call his name Jesus, for he will save his people from their sins" (Matthew 1:21).

The name 'Jesus' in English has a complicated linguistic history. 'Jesus' is an Anglicized form of the Greek name Yesous found in the New Testament. Yesous represents the Hebrew Bible name Yeshua, (which occurs as 'Jeshua' in English Bibles). In the Hebrew Bible 'Yeho-' is used at the beginning of certain proper names e.g. Jehoshaphat, and Yehoshua is a form of the Hebrew verb 'yasha' which means to deliver, save, or rescue. Therefore, the name Jesus, in Hebrew, means 'God saves'. Hence the angel Gabriel when announcing that the baby was to be called Jesus was not only giving him his proper name but one which expressed both his identity and his mission. This was confirmed in Joseph's dream when the reason was given for calling the baby Jesus was, 'he will save his people from their sins' (Matthew 1:21). No wonder the angel Gabriel began his message to Mary with the words 'rejoice'. There was much to rejoice about, God, our God, was going to come live among us, as one of us, but with a special mission, that to save us from our sins, our shortcomings, our failures. However, Mary's response is not one of joy but a very practical one, not an emotional one, "But how can this come about, since I am a virgin?" (Luke 1:34)

Mary's words were followed by a total surrender in humility to the will of God, "'I am the handmaid of the Lord,' said Mary, let what you have said be done to me" (Luke 1:38). First, there is the humility and then there is the joy expressed when Mary goes to meet her cousin Elizabeth, Zachariah's wife and initially a barren woman; who had just been told that she in her old age would bear a son: that son who would become known as John the Baptist. "Mary set out at that time and went as quickly as she could to a town in the hill country of Judah. She went into Zechariah's house and greeted Elizabeth. Now as soon as Elizabeth heard Mary's greeting the child, leapt in her womb and Elizabeth was filled with the Holy Spirit" (Luke 1:39-42). Elizabeth exclaimed (to Mary); "Of all women you are the most blessed and blessed is the fruit of your womb, (1:42) For the moment your greeting reached my ears, the child in my womb leapt for joy" (1–44). Mary's response, which is known as the Magnificat (the Latin verb for glorifies) is similar to that of many of the Psalms in its language and form. It is powerful in its humility and begins by rejoicing in an all-merciful, all-tender, all-loving God, who answers prayers.

Mary began with the prayer, "My soul proclaims the greatness of the Lord And exults in God my Saviour;" echoing the words spoken by Hannah in The Song of Hannah (1 Samuel 2:1–10). When Hannah's prayer had been heard and answered, she exclaimed joyfully, "My heart exults in the LORD! The LORD has made me strong."

Mary, in her exultation, continues; "And His mercy reaches from age to age for those who fear Him. He has shown the power of his arm. He has routed the proud heart. He has pulled down princes from their mighty thrones and exalted the lowly. The hungry he has filled with good things. The rich he has sent empty away. He has come to the help of Israel his servant, mindful of his mercy-according to the promise he made to our ancestors – of his mercy to Abraham and his descendants."

Thus the Magnificat can be summed up in three words: humility, prayerfulness, and obedience. In the Magnificat, Mary teaches us how to pray, three basic ingredients we need if we are to lead a joyful, Christian life. How appropriate Mary's prayer should come at the beginning of the Christian story.

As the Christmas story unfolds, there is a tendency to reflect on the birth, on the incarnation, God becoming man, and often the fact that Jesus came to save us from our sins gets overlooked. This is the message that was given to the shepherds in the fields nearby, looking after their sheep, "The angel of the Lord appeared to them (shepherds), and the glory of the Lord shone around them. They were terrified, but the angel said, 'Do not be afraid. Listen, I bring you news of great joy, a joy to be shared by the whole people. Today in the town of David a saviour has been born to you; he is Christ the Lord'" (Luke 2:9-10). However, the key words now are, ('a joy') to be shared with all people, again reinforcing the message that this joy is caused because God, our Father, has seen us in a pitiful state and has come among us, to help us, to teach us about love, to remove the barrier separating us from Him.

Jesus came to set us free, release us from the bondage that prevents us from leading a joyful Christian life. This news was announced first of all to the shepherds, who were living out in the fields nearby, engaged in their occupation of being watchful, for although it was night-time, in the darkness there lurked many dangers. It was to these poor, marginalised groups of people, living in the darkness that the brightness of an angel appeared and, 'glory shone around them' (Luke 2: 9). The night was lit up with brightness, the darkness dispelled. The shepherd's reaction was not one of joy but of fear, they quite understandably, 'became afraid'. People who were used to existing in the darkness were suddenly challenged but instead of running away, they stayed and listened to the news, although their understanding could only have been limited. Indeed they were rewarded for their trust for as they were looking upwards, listening to the message, "Suddenly with the angel there was a great throng of the heavenly host, praising God" (Luke 2:13).

When the angels had gone, the shepherds were united; people who normally would not have communicated, partly because they would have been looking after their sheep in different places, were suddenly speaking to one another. But not only that; they were agreeing as a group on how to go forward, to discover more about what the messenger of the Lord had told them. They believed in the message of the birth of a saviour, as revealed to them. "Let us go to Bethlehem and see these things that have happened which the Lord has made known to us" (Luke 2:15). God had met them, where they were and revealed Himself to them. They responded and set out on their journey, in faith and trust, with hope in their hearts. They were not disappointed. In return for their faithfulness, they became a very powerful witness. "When they saw the child, they repeated what they had been told about him, and everyone who heard it was astonished at what the shepherds had to say" (Luke 18:19). However, it was not just those around who were touched by their revelations. Mary was also, "As for Mary, she treasured all these things and pondered them in her heart" (Luke 2:19-20). Mary who had just become the mother of God received confirmation on a personal level of what she had already received on a spiritual level. She witnessed the joy on the faces of those shepherds, as they looked at the baby she had just borne. They had come out of the darkness, into the light, experienced the joy and went back "Glorifying and praising God for all they had heard and seen, it was exactly as they had been told" (Luke 2:20).

In contrast to the poor shepherds tending their sheep in darkness, there was another group of people who, with prior knowledge, had also set out on a journey of discovery. However, this time, they were following a star. These were the magi or wise men. There is no mention of them in Luke's gospel but in Matthew's they are referred to as 'some wise men who came from the east', or in some bibles they are referred to as the 'magi' (Matthew 2:2, NIV). Magi were astrologers, who would have been advisers to kings. They combined their insights, which were devised from sophisticated astronomical observations, with interpretations based on prior knowledge. Although they were not Jewish, they had apparently studied the Hebrew Scriptures and found there a clear transcript of truth, for according to Balaam: "A Star from Jacob shall take the leadership; a sceptre arises from Israel" (Numbers 24:17). And according to the prophecy of Micah: "But you, (Bethlehem) Ephrathah, the least of the clans of Judah, out of you will be born for me the one who is to rule over Israel" (Micah 5:2). So unlike the Shepherds, they were rich, educated and Gentiles. Although with both groups, the numbers are unspecified, it is generally assumed that there were three wise men because, in Luke's gospel, three gifts are mentioned; gold frankincense and myrrh.

Three is quite a significant number. The Pythagoreans taught that the number three was the first true number. Three is the number of times: past, present, future; birth, life, death; beginning, middle, end, and is considered the number of harmonies, wisdom and understanding. In the Bible, the number three is quite a significant number. The main association of the three is with the Trinity: the Father, the Son, and the Holy Spirit. In the Old Testament, there were three righteous patriarchs before the flood: Abel, Enoch, and Noah; while after the deluge there was the righteous 'fathers': Abraham, Isaac, and Jacob. In the New Testament, there were three disciples, who witnessed the Transfiguration: Peter, James, and John.

In addition to this, the third letter of the Hebrew alphabet is the Gimmel; one of its primary meanings is endurance, while the main meaning is to nourish until completely ripe. Its noun form means a camel, primarily because the camel can endure long trips through the desert without drinking water. The Gimmel teaches that two opposing forces must be blended to form a third more complete and perfect entity. To accomplish all of this takes endurance. Indeed the Gimmel could be used to describe the journey taken by the wise men, with their camels. They had set off on their quest not only with knowledge, but also with a desire to see the Messiah, who was outside their realm of belief, and through endurance and perseverance, were led to the stable. "The star halted over the place where the child was. At the sign, which was the sight of the star, static in the night sky, above the place where Jesus was born, they were filled with delight" (Matthew 2: 9–10), their journey had come to an end. The sufferings and hardships they had endured were over and they had accomplished their mission. Their joy was compounded with humility because they went into the house and, "Saw the child with his mother, Mary, and falling on their knees they did him homage" (Matthew 2:11). Their journey to seek the truth had led them to encounter the baby, Jesus the messiah. Thus the birth of Jesus who was born for all, (John 10:10) who had come into the world for both Jews and Gentiles, so that, 'all may have life and have it abundantly' (10:10) began with what could be described as an explosion of joy, both in heaven and on earth.

It wasn't just at birth that there were experiences of joy. Throughout the ministry of Jesus, there are references to joy. Indeed Jesus took great joy in His mission, "These things I have spoken to you so that My joy may be in you, and that your joy may be made full" (John 15:11). "At that very time, He rejoiced greatly in the Holy Spirit, and said, 'I praise You, O Father, Lord of heaven and earth, that You have hidden these things from the wise and intelligent and have revealed them to infants. Yes, Father, for this way was well-pleasing in Your sight'" (Luke 10:21). It was not only Jesus who expressed joy. In Matthew's Gospel, reference is made to the Prophecy of Isaiah by Jesus as He begins his public ministry, "Here is My servant, whom I have chosen, My beloved, in whom My soul delights. I have endowed him with My spirit, and he will bring true justice to the nations" (Matthew 12:18). This is the second time joy by God, the Father is mentioned. In Matthew's gospel at the Baptism of Jesus, we are told, "And a voice from heaven said, 'This is my dearly loved Son, who brings me great joy'" (Matthew 4:17).

Therefore, as spirit-filled Christians, we should be filled with joy but in our everyday lives that just does not happen; we don't go around feeling that joy bubble up inside us. I suppose we are just like the flag bearers. They wouldn't have felt joy in their everyday struggles, their suffering, and the sacrifices, and so it is with us. We need also to experience this paradox, of suffering bringing joy, and this is exactly what happened at the end of Jesus' ministry.

The night before he was crucified, after the last supper, Jesus went into the Garden of Gethsemane and took with him Peter, James, and John, the same three disciples who had witnessed the Transfiguration. However, unlike the

Transfiguration, where Jesus had revealed himself in radiant glory (Matthew 17:2 and Mark 9:2–3), in the Garden of Gethsemane was a completely different Jesus, one whose state of mind could be described as that of despair. With the three disciples, he didn't try to put on a show, a pretence, a good, 'spiritual looking' front for them. He was honest with them about how bad he was feeling and so he asked Peter, James, and John to pray with him. Jesus knew what it was that God wanted him to do, but he didn't want to do it. There was a conflict here between the will of God and the will of Jesus and His words reveal this, "Father, if you are willing, take this cup from me; yet not my will, but yours be done" (Luke 22:42). The 'cup' that he asked God to let pass from him was his death. Thus, what has now become known as the agony in the garden was this dilemma of Jesus. He wanted to obey God, but he didn't want to die. He wanted God to save him from death. However, if this was not to be then 'Amen', so be it. In his agony, in his despair, God, his father, did answer him. "Then an angel appeared to him, coming from heaven to give him strength" (Luke 22:44). This strength allowed Him to go obediently to His disfiguring, humiliating, cruel, death. A death He did not deserve for He had done nothing wrong but one which He undertook to complete His mission, here on earth, to save us from the consequences of our sins, to reunite us with God, our Father. Was the strength given to Jesus was that of acceptance with joy, knowing all the suffering, was suffering to be endured for a short time, the death on the cross which would bring him closer to his father, doing his will so that when it was ended he would be seated at God's right hand, with the Father he adored?

We can also learn the lesson of acceptance with joy. When people insult us, ignore us, belittle us, instead of retaliating, we can bring our hurts, our pains, and sufferings to the foot of the cross, not begrudgingly, or with a long face, feeling sorry for ourselves but with an acceptance of joy, knowing as Jesus did that his suffering brought him closer to his father's heart, the ultimate lesson in love. The paradox of suffering is turned into joy.

This paradox continues for us when we contemplate the cross. It may seem impossible to feel joy at the sight of Jesus on the cross, knowing that he suffered and died for 'me', for 'my sins', and He did it because 'He loves me'. Indeed, we can't feel spiritual joy when we are in denial of our sins, in a state of unrepentance. We need to stand at the foot of the cross, look up into the face of Jesus, so filled with love and concern for us, and from our heart, whisper the words, "I'm sorry" for when we whisper there is a tendency to draw close to the person we are whispering to, and they, in turn, will draw close to us. We can then move forward and feel the power of the cross; the empty cross, the sign of victory over death, over sin. After all, the suffering of the cross came the joy of the Resurrection.

As Luke's gospel highlighted the joy of the Annunciation, it is John's gospel which highlights the joy in the Resurrection, "In the evening of that same day, the first day of the week, the doors were closed in the room where the disciples were, for fear of the Jews. Jesus came and stood among them. He said to them, 'Peace be with you,' and showed them his hands and his side. The disciples were filled with joy when they saw the Lord, and he said to them again, 'Peace be with you'" (John: 19–21).

The disciples had been told that Jesus had risen, and John's gospel gives us an account of what happened. After Mary Magdala had gone to the tomb and had seen the stone had been moved she went running to Simon Peter. "So Peter set out with the other disciple (John) to go to the tomb. They ran together, but the other disciple, running faster than Peter, reached the tomb first; he bent down and saw the linen cloth lying on the ground, but did not go in" (John 20:3–6). However, Peter following him, "went right into the tomb" (John 20:6). Instead of rushing into the empty tomb, John stopped, paused, reflected, and then noticed the precise position of the clothes in the tomb. Was John trying to make sense of what he was seeing? He noted that Jesus had left the clothes without disturbing them, and indirectly was making a comparison with the death of Lazarus, as he had left the grave with the grave clothes still wrapped around him. It was after the pause, the reflection that, "The other disciple who had reached the tomb first also went in; he saw, and he believed" (John 20:9). That short time of reflection allowed the Holy Spirit to bring to mind all that Jesus had said about His death and resurrection, and so John was able to embrace the empty tomb with increased and unshakeable faith. However, this was not the case with the rest of the disciples.

After the death of Jesus, although there were definite signs that all Jesus had said to the disciples before the crucifixion, was happening but they had great difficulty in believing. They still had trouble believing that Jesus was truly the Messiah. The phrase 'too good to be true' springs to mind. Although Jesus had told them that he would die and in three days rise again from the dead, they had thought he was speaking metaphorically. After all is said and done, they had been ordinary, mostly uneducated men, who had responded to the call of Jesus, who had chosen to follow him. When they were challenged with the suffering and death, of Jesus, the doubts, and the fears had resurfaced. They were afraid to allow themselves to believe as they had also greatly suffered from Jesus at the crucifixion. It wasn't until they met Him, face to face, had a personal encounter, with the Risen Jesus that they experienced the joy and the power of the Resurrection. When Moses held up the bronze serpent in the desert, all the Israelites who had been bitten by serpents, instead of fearing death, could look at the serpent and receive life, be healed, and be brought back into harmony with God. Now, this too could happen to both Jews and Gentiles, for when they looked at the Resurrected Jesus, they too could be brought back into life, into harmony with God the Father. They also could 'rejoice' for the Light had dispelled the darkness. As Isaiah had prophesied, "For you shall go out in joy and be led forth in peace; the mountains and the hills before you shall break forth into singing, and all the trees of the field shall clap their hands" Isaiah (55:12).

We too, like the flagbearers, can turn our sufferings in our spiritual life, our endurance; our setbacks into victory. A victory expressed in joy! With tears of joy we can encounter and meet our saviour but only through the power of the Holy Spirit and then with confidence, we know that joy will continue throughout our spiritual life if we but only stay faithfully true to the Spirit while we strive to live in the third fruit of the Spirit – peace.

Chapter Two
Peace

"Peace I bequeath to you; my own peace I give you. A peace the world cannot give, this is my gift to you" (John 14:27).

'Give peace a chance' was very much an anthem of the 1960s, coined by John Lenin and Yoko Ono. Their call was not only for world peace, which encompassed a concept of harmony by an absence of hostility but had a much higher, deeper sense of peace, one which needed to begin by finding inner peace, within oneself. To achieve this inner peace, meditation was encouraged; as inner peace is believed to be a state of consciousness or enlightenment that can be achieved by various types of meditation, prayer, *t'ai chi ch'uan*, yoga, or other various types of mental or physical disciplines. Quite simply, it is a means by which one comes to know oneself.

Inner peace or what is sometimes referred to as 'peace of mind', therefore, refers to a state of being internally, spiritually at peace; to be sufficiently and understanding to be able to keep calm in the face of apparent discord or stress. Within the meditative traditions, the psychological or inward achievement of 'peace of mind' is often associated with bliss and happiness.

The Christian, however, can also achieve a very high sense of inner peace, which cannot be achieved through the practices of the world or chemical aids, but only from Jesus Himself, through His most Holy Spirit. Thus Christians, empowered by the Holy Spirit, can reach a deep peace of mind, serenity, and calmness, in the face of adversity. Jesus spoke of peace as His gift to us, but unlike the gifts of the Holy Spirit which are used to strengthen and enlighten the path of fellow Christians, peace is one of the fruits of the Holy Spirit; it is used to strengthen and enlighten us. Just like joy, peace springs from within, and like the branches of the vine can spread, given the right nourishment and conditions. Therefore, to develop a more comprehensive understanding of the term peace; how we can find peace within ourselves and how we can be instruments of peace to others, we need to turn to the word of God, which holds all the answers and is filled with verses that can bring peace in the middle of struggles, worries and fears, if we but seek them.

In both the Old and New Testament, various forms of the word *peace* are found, over four hundred times, (depending on the version of the Bible), which include inner peace, peace with God, peace with fellow man, and even false peace. The Hebrew word for peace is Shalom, and according to 'Jews for Jesus', the word 'shalom' occurs more than two hundred and fifty times in the Tanakh (Hebrew Bible) and appears in two hundred and thirteen separate verses. It has a wide range of meanings which include: harmony, wholeness, completeness, and tranquillity – especially tranquillity of the soul. Shalom is derived from a Hebrew root word denoting wholeness or completeness and means entering into a state of wholeness and unity, to restore or in a right relationship, whether it be with God, man, or with ourselves.

According to the Dali Lama, we can never find peace in the outer world until we make peace with ourselves. As the well-known hymn says, "Let there be peace on earth and let it begin with me" (written by Jill Jackson-Miller and Sy Miller in 1955). Inner peace, or peace of mind, is like joy, it causes us to think and behave in a positive way. It is not, as is often supposed, the absence of conflict from life, but the ability to cope with it. We need to be united within ourselves and not have areas of conflict, especially within our thinking, our thoughts. While we are being torn or pulled in different directions, there can be no feeling of calm and tranquilly. The old expression, 'I can't decide as I'm in two minds' is a good example of the dilemmas that we often face, that which causes us to become divided within ourselves; and which makes us feel we are incomplete. Normally, this is because we don't have enough knowledge about the subject, but it could also be due to a deep inner negative emotion that we are not aware of and have buried deep within our subconscious. There are many ways we experience a lack of peace of mind, and we need to take time to be reflective, to come to know ourselves; we need to spend time in silence.

One of the main causes for lack of peace is noise. 'I can't hear myself think' is a well-known saying but it is very true. In the poem, Desiderata, Max Ehrmann, reminds us of the connection between peace and silence, 'Go placidly amid the noise and haste, and remember what peace there may be in silence'. C. S Lewis goes even further with the dangers of lack of silence in the book 'Screwtape Letters'. The senior demon, Screwtape, reveals one very interesting plan of the devil. To drive us away from God, Satan chooses to distract us with, 'noise'. He knows that if we are overrun by countless distractions we will be unable to hear the voice of God in silence.

Noise is like darkness concealing the truth, distracting us. In our world, today silence has been buried deep beneath a cacophony of sounds, television, radio, music, machinery, transport, iPhones and so the list continues. They have become so commonplace in our lives that we tend to downgrade and refer to them as background noise. However, noise can be quite dangerous in our lives. Regular exposure, to consistently elevated sound levels, or noise pollution as it is referred to, is detrimental to both our physical and psychological health. Through extensive research, the noise had been attributed to causing hypertension, high-stress levels, tinnitus, hearing loss, sleep disturbances. It is not surprising therefore that loud noises or continual noise affects not only our health, but also our behaviour in a negative way, and can consequently rob us of our calmness, our serenity which is to be found in silence.

Controversially though, it is silence we have come to view negatively, relating it with sadness or loneliness. Indeed, we have even become afraid of silence. And yet it is this lack of noise, or silence, which allows us to enter into a deep communication not only within ourselves but equally importantly, with each other. We are social creatures and to function properly, we need to be able to communicate effectively at different levels. When we are communicating effectively, we can be silent, thereby allowing us not only to respond to what the person is saying but also in the silent pause to be not only aware of the spoken word but to be able to read the body language. Approximately seventy to eighty percent of what is communicated is non-verbal. In silence, voice inflexions, tonality changes, facial gestures, and other body cues, can all be experienced. It is this non-verbal communication that allows us to 'hear with our eyes', and so respond appropriately. It permits dialogue not monologue and allows us to hear what the person is not saying. Indeed, we need to be observers, listening with our eyes.

Therefore to achieve proper dialogue leading to peace of mind we need to be tuned in to what is happening, not only what is being said, but why it is being said; we need to be reflective. One of the dangers of using social media to communicate is we are avoiding the issue of interacting face to face, and consequently causing ineffectual communication. Words can have a very negative impact on our perception of ourselves, if taken at face value and that is why bullying has become such a problem, especially on social media. Unfortunately, the person being bullied remains, 'silent' but not reflective. There is, "a time to be silent and a time to speak" (Ecclesiastes 3:7). Communication of negative feelings needs to be shared, with the appropriate people. They should never be buried but need to be brought out into the light, into the open. However, cruel and spiteful behaviour does not only exist on social media but unfortunately can also occur within our social groups, with work colleagues, school friends etc. and even within our churches, our Christian gatherings.

Everyone wants peace and unity these days even if it means peace at all costs. Whether it is in our world, within our societies, our family, even our Christian communities, we have become good at pretending that everything is 'fine' in the name of 'live and let live', even though it means compromising the truth. However, there is peace and there is a false peace. Just because we may not be in conflict does not mean there is peace. Pope Francis spoke about false peace when he greeted the pilgrims in St. Peters Square (April 16, 2014). He stressed the importance of knowing how to tell the difference between peace from God, and the false peace offered by the devil. "True peace," he claimed, "always comes from Jesus, and is sometimes 'wrapped' in the cross, while the other, false peace that only makes you 'kind of happy' comes from the devil." According to Pope Francis, we need 'grace': a word which when used in the New Testament comes from the Greek word *'charis'*, which means 'God's favour, blessing, or kindness': this will help us to distinguish between true and false peace. He explained that while on the outside we might think everything is okay and that we're doing good, "Way down inside is the devil. The devil always destroys. He tells you this is the way and then leaves you alone," he continued, adding that the devil is "a poor payer; he always rips you off".

Saint Paul in his First Epistle to Timothy, wrote a warning of being led astray into a false sense of security, in his First Epistle to Timothy (4:1–2): "Now the Spirit explicitly says that in the last times some will turn away from the faith by paying attention to deceitful spirits and demonic instructions through the hypocrisy of liars with branded consciences." However, it is in his second letter to Timothy where Paul, leaves no stone unturned by his warnings. "You may be quite sure that in the last days there are going to be some difficult times. People will be self-centred and grasping, boastful, arrogant, and rude, disobedient to their parents, ungrateful,

43

irreligious, heartless, and unappeasable; they will be slanderous, profligates, savages, and enemies of everything that is good; they will be treacherous and reckless, conceited, and demented by pride, preferring their own pleasure to God. They will keep up the outward appearance of religion but have rejected the inner power of it. Have nothing to do with people like that"(2 Tim 3:1–5). Paul thus lists nineteen characteristics, with 'lovers of themselves' and 'lovers of pleasure rather than lovers of God' serving as bookends containing the others within them.

It must be remembered that because we are in a church or Christian setting does not mean that everyone will behave as Christians. I remember being in a church where the priest had to remind the women not to leave their handbags on the seat when they came up to receive Holy Communion, as several bags had been stolen. Just because they were in a church didn't mean they were safe, that someone wasn't going to steal them. It didn't have to be a thief from the outside, who had come in on the off chance but it could also have been someone within the church who was having financial problems, had been praying about their situation and had suddenly seen an unattended bag as an answer to prayer. After all, God does work in mysterious ways! Just as the person who had mistakenly taken the handbag, thinking it was a gift from God so too a Christians may act erroneously believing that they are responding to God's providence.

We should not be lulled into a false sense of security, for if so, we may not be able to achieve peace of mind. A time to be silent and a time to speak does not only apply to social media but needs to become a part of our daily lives. We need to develop reflective silences which will impact all areas of our life as a means of achieving the deeper goal of inner peace. People can steal our peace of mind without us being aware of it, and one such way is telling us negative comments people are supposed to have said about us. I have even heard professional people saying to their staff. "Come and say to my face what you are saying behind my back." Which raises the question, how do you know people are talking behind your back? Jesus demonstrates how to deal with a similar situation where negative comments were made about another person, "Now Martha, who was distracted with all the serving, said, 'Lord do you not care that my sister is leaving me to do the serving all by myself? Please tell her to help me.'" Inadvertently, she was drawing Jesus into a confrontational situation, making him take sides, and act on her behalf. However, Jesus responded with a gentle rebuke. "Martha, Martha" and by the double use of her name, Jesus stresses the importance of what he is going to say, "You worry and fret about so many things, and yet few are needed, indeed only one. It is Mary who has chosen the better part; it is not to be taken from her" (Luke 10:42). Instead of rebuking Mary, Jesus used the opportunity to point out to Martha that the words she used showed where her priorities lay. They illuminated her problems. Indeed, Jesus acted as Isaiah prophesied, "He will not judge by appearance nor make a decision based on hearsay." Through His reply, Jesus also reinforced the importance that one honours Him more by listening to him than by rushing around ministering to his needs. We need to listen to Jesus, not other people. We need to cultivate the silences so that we can produce the fruit of peace.

'Fools rush in where angels fear to tread', first written by Alexander Pope in his poem 'An Essay on Criticism' is a very familiar saying and is used in different circumstances but can equally apply in conversations, especially when there is a silence, a gap, when a person jumps in expressing their views, their opinions. However, their words and actions can be a lot, a lot more than just avoiding silences. Instead, such people will often disrupt the silence and have become very adept at drawing the attention, the limelight, back to themselves. They seem to be unaware of what is being said, but more importantly, they refuse to observe the body language, and they misuse the pauses. Not only can they be exceedingly irritating, but they can also be quite destructive, especially within a Christian sharing group, as they seem to use every opportunity to promote themselves, by pursuing their agendas. All this in spite of the fact that Jesus Himself warned us of such behaviour. "Be careful not to parade your good deeds before men to attract their notice; by doing this, you will lose all reward from your Father in heaven" (Matthew6:1–2).

Unfortunately, people who act in this way are not hard to find as they are the ones who always like to draw the conversation back to themselves; to try and show off intellectually but pushing forward their views, their beliefs, with all their sentences beginning with, 'I think; I feel; I believe; in my opinion' etc. In the worst-case scenario, they will use the Gospel to build themselves up while they tear others down; and all done in a gentle, subtle way normally while they are smiling, or using a very gentle tone of voice. We are immediately aware when a tone becomes aggressive and sit up alert, but gentleness can be deceiving. Therefore, it is important to take time to be reflective, to develop an awareness of discrepancies of body language, words, and tones. If we are unaware of what is happening we could be walking around wounded, allowing conflict within ourselves, but we could be allowing others to also suffer at their hands.

Jesus did warn us to "beware of sheep in wolves clothing" (Matthew 7:15) and it was not just false we prophets that were being referred to but also so-called followers of Christ. Because a person claims that they belong to Jesus does not mean that they follow the rules, in that, they behave in a Christian way. As James in his letter explained, "Remember this, my dear brothers: be *quick* to *listen* but *slow* to *speak* and (consequently) slow to rouse your temper" (1:19) and again he warned, "Nobody must imagine that he is religious while he still goes on deceiving himself and not keeping control over his tongue; anyone who does this has the wrong idea of religion" (1:26). Therefore, it is so important then to take time out in silence and as in any difficult situation, seek guidance from the Holy Spirit by listening to His voice. Once we have knowledge and insight, then we can rationalise what exactly the problem is and with whom it lies. We can then start to reclaim our inner peace.

Indeed silence helps us not only to find inner peace, especially in stressful situations but it also allows us to communicate more effectively with God, our Father, through the Holy Spirit of the risen Jesus. Jesus throughout His ministry often went off by himself to talk to His father. "His reputation continued to grow, and large crowds would gather to hear him and to have their sickness cured but he would always go off to someplace where he could be alone and pray" (Luke: 15-17). "In the morning, long before dawn, he got up and left the house and went off to a lonely place and prayed there" (Mark 1:35). "Now it was about this time that he went out into the hills to pray, and he spent the whole night in prayer to God" (Luke 6:12). And of course on the night of the Last Supper, "He (Jesus) then left to make his way as usual to the Mount of Olives, with the disciples following. When they reached the place he said to them, 'pray not to be put to the test'. Then he withdrew from them, about a stone's throw away and knelt down and prayed" (Luke 22:39-40). It is when we too are distressed, deeply troubled and are suffering trials we too need to withdraw and talk to Our Father, just as Jesus did, right from the heart. At the end of the prayer, Jesus was at peace. He had peace of mind as He was doing the Father's will, obedient even to death, death on the cross (Philippians: 2:8). His situation hadn't changed; there were still the trials, sufferings, even the death, but through prayer what had changed was Jesus's inner peace; confirmation of His Father's will and total trust, which led to acceptance, and acceptance with joy! When we can pray that prayer of surrender that Jesus prayed, "Father if you are willing, take this cup away from me. Nevertheless, let your will be done not mine" (Luke 22:42-43), and if possible, pray with an acceptance of joy then we too can achieve that peace which Jesus gave us. "Peace I bequeath to you; my own peace I give you. A peace the world cannot give, this is my gift to you" (John 14:27).

Jesus also addressed the issue of how to pray, not only in our words but also in our actions, in the Sermon on the Mount "And when you pray, do not imitate the hypocrites, they love to say their prayers standing up in the synagogues and at the street corners for people to see them – but when you pray go to your private room and when you have shut your door, pray to your Father who is in that secret place, and your Father who sees all that is done in secret will reward you" (Matthew 6:5-6). Being alone allows us to be free from distractions so we can enter into dialogue, to be able to not only talk but more importantly to listen. This is something Jesus would have been very aware of, listening to His Father. "I call you friends because I have made known to you everyone I have learnt (heard) from my Father" (John 15:15). It is only in the stillness, the silence, can we hear God speaking to us. "After the earthquake came a fire. But Yahweh was not in the fire. And after the fire there came the sound of a gentle breeze, or as in some versions, 'a still male voice'. And when Elijah heard this, he covered his face with his cloak and went out and stood at the entrance of the cave. Then a voice came to him; "the small voice of God" (1Kings 19:12-14). In today's busy life it is not easy building in a quiet time, to listen to the voice of God. If we desire inner peace then we need to practice stillness in both heart and mind, to be able to hear the quiet voice of the Lord.

As God speaks to us gently in whispers, through the Holy Spirit, we need to be in silence to hear Him. As Mother Teresa stated, in the 'Heart of the World: Thoughts, Stories and Prayers', "In the silence of the heart God speaks. If you face God in prayer and silence, God will speak to you. Then you will know that you are nothing. It is only when you realize your nothingness, your emptiness, that God can fill you with Himself. Souls of prayer are souls of great silence." Although in many of our Christian gatherings there is much evidence of the Holy Spirit working, especially in the joyful praise, it is only in the silence that we can hear Him. After all the Holy

49

Spirit is often depicted as a dove, a gentle bird. I once heard someone talk about their pet bird, a dove. They said that the dove was trained to come and sit on their shoulder but if there was a sudden loud noise or voices, it would immediately fly away, as it was a very timid and gentle bird, associated more with peace than with aggression.

Perhaps, therefore, it is no coincidence that the dove, from the time of Noah, has been a very powerful symbol of peace. One of the principles of interpretation of the Bible (Bible hermeneutics) is the law of the first mention. Quite simply this means that the first time a word occurs in the Scriptures it is scrutinised, analysed and it is interpreted, which in turn gives the key to understanding its meaning in every other place. Thus the dove and olive branch being a symbol of peace comes from the story of Noah, in the book of Genesis. "At the end of forty days, Noah opened the porthole he had made in the ark, and he sent out the raven. This went off and flew back and forth until the waters dried up from the earth. Then he sent out a dove, to see whether the waters were receding from the surface of the earth. The dove finding nowhere to perch, returned to him in the ark, for there was water over the whole surface of the earth; putting out his hand he took hold of it and brought it back into the ark with him. After waiting seven more days, again he sent out the dove from the ark. In the evening, the dove came back to him and there it was with a new olive branch in its beak" (Genesis 8:6–11).

Thus the dove bringing back the olive branch was seen as much more than just evidence that the water had receded but has become one of the most ancient symbols of peace and also a symbol of new beginnings. There have been many discussions about Noah's choice of birds, the dove, and the raven. Followers of Philo of Alexandria, a Hellenistic Jewish philosopher, argued that the birds were purely symbolic; the raven representing vice, as it is a scavenger, feeding on the carcases of animals and so would have been comfortable in the destroyed world; while the dove representing virtue could not bear to live in the destroyed world. However, another trend of thought is that Noah would have been acquainted with the difference in their nature; in that the raven in seeking its food settles upon every carcase that it sees, whereas the dove will only settle upon that which is dry and clean. In addition to this comparison between the birds' nature, there is also the contrast of is the colour of their plumage; the raven being black whereas the dove is white, thus noting the contrast of light and darkness. Consequently, in the Old Testament, the dove is seen as a bird that brings peace out of conflict; renewal out of destruction or destructive situations; illuminating the darkness with light; giving, hope, and life. How apt than the symbol for the Holy Spirit, in the New Testament, should be the dove.

The dove became the symbol of the Holy Spirit after being mentioned in the Baptism of Jesus. "As soon as Jesus was baptised he came up from the water, and suddenly the heavens opened, and he saw the Spirit of God descending like a dove and coming down on him. And a voice spoke from heaven, 'This is my Son, the Beloved, my favour rests on him'" (Matthew 3:16–17). There is a similar account in Mark's gospel. "It was at this time that Jesus came from Nazareth in Galilee and was baptised in the Jordan by John. No sooner had he come up from the water than he saw the heavens torn apart and the Spirit, like a dove, descending on him. And a voice came from heaven, 'You are my Son, the Beloved; my favour rests on you'" (Mark 1:9–11). While Luke writes, "Now when all the people had been baptised and while Jesus after his own baptism was at prayer, heaven opened and the Holy Spirit descended on him in bodily shape, like a dove. And a voice came from heaven, 'You are my Son, the Beloved; my favour rests on you.'" The same account of the opening of the skies is part of the Old Testament picture of God descending, but here it is the Spirit which comes down, like a dove – the symbol of gentleness and peace, uniting heaven, and earth.

The beginning of the ministry of Jesus which began in a peaceful, gentle way, was, quite ironically, to end violently. Jesus who gave his life to protect us, provide for us, sustain us, and bring us rest suffered a violent death to bring us peace. Quite a paradox but in Jesus' death, peace was established, just as there cannot be peace until the end of the war. War brings peace and peace cannot be established while war is raging. Even in the Hebrew alphabet, the seventh letter the Zayin which is a symbol of peace is shaped like a sword. It is generally accepted that weapons are used to bring peace from those who are opposing them. As it is the seventh letter, it has always been regarded in the Jewish tradition as enjoying wholeness, completeness; one of the meanings of Shalom. The way the actual letter is formed gives rise to the interpretation of the design as a crown and a sceptre. The Zayin thus alludes to power and authority. The 'Hebrew for Christian' website uses this interpretation to link the crown with Jesus, the Messiah, the King of the Jews. As the Zayin also represents a sword it is showing Jesus equipped with the Holy Spirit and so for the Christian, the Zayin can be interpreted as the Holy Spirit bringing peace.

However, just as there is false peace within our lives so there can be false peace within our world, and we need to be not only aware of it but use it constructively to inform our prayers, our actions. Because there is no war, or conflicts happening in our neighbourhood does not mean we can adopt the attitude of indifference. We should never turn a blind eye to injustice or the sufferings of others. We cannot refuse to notice the desperation in the eyes of the refugees as they flee their war-torn country, clutching their dying children to their breasts: Keep silent when the marginalised are being downtrodden: Agree to appeasement. After all the famous words of Neville Chamberlin, 'Peace in our time', was followed months later by war. Appeasement for peace's sake doesn't work. We may sweep the dirt under the carpet, but it won't go away, it is still there. It needs to be dealt with properly. That is why Jesus said, "No one sews a piece of unshrunken cloth on an old cloak; if he does, the patch pulls away from it, the new from the old, and the tear gets worse. And nobody puts new wine into old wineskins; if he does the wine will burst the skins, and the wine is lost and the skins too. No new wine, fresh skins" (Mark 2: 21–23). Sticking plasters on an open wound just doesn't work! If we want true peace, we need to treat the cause and not just the symptoms. We need help.

And that is why Jesus came and brought peace to the earth and through His Holy Spirit, this peace can continue in each of us. "I have said these things to you while still with you; but the Advocate, the Holy Spirit, whom the Father will send in my name, will teach you everything and remind you of all I have said to you. Peace, I bequeath to you, my own peace I give you, a peace that the world cannot give, this is my gift to you. Do not let your hearts be troubled or afraid"(John 14: 25-28). With total faith, we can claim this peace and then when we pray for peace, the peace that is so needed within our societies, our world, will be given to us. However, if we allow ourselves to enter into the suffering of those in war-torn countries, then how much more powerful our prayers for peace will be, as they come straight from the heart. United with the Holy Spirit, the dove of peace we can join our hearts with Jesus and pray for all my live-in peace.

Just as joy can be experienced through suffering and hardships so too can peace be achieved through conflict and battles. Peace just doesn't happen. Life involves hardships, greed, and aggression thus we need to learn how to live victorious, to overcome the negativity with positivity. To do this, we need to strive to achieve peace in our lives, a peace that brings inner tranquillity and harmony. Quite simply, we need to live the life of the Christian whose trust, total trust, is in the Godhead, the Father, the Son, and the Holy Spirit. Then we can sing, from our hearts the hymn, "Let there be peace on earth and let it begin with me." (Let There Be Peace. Hymn unknown.)

Chapter Three
Patience

"Be quiet before Yahweh and wait patiently for him" (Psalm 37:7).

"Let your hope keep you joyful, be patient in your troubles, and pray at all times (Romans 12:12)"

'God grant me patience but please do it quickly', is a saying that became popular a few years ago and yes, there is a certain element of truth in it. Deep down, how many of us can deny that this is a prayer we can relate to and one we would often have prayed. Living in our world, today has taken its toll on us and our patience. Comparisons between life today and one hundred years ago are staggering when the time taken in travel, communication, commerce, buildings, etc. are taken into account. There can be no arguing to the fact that the pace of life today is fast and furious, so consequently we have become carried along on a tide of expectations, expecting to achieve yesterday what we should achieve tomorrow, one of the challenges of living in the twenty-first century.

Patience involves waiting, and waiting is just like silence, has negative connotations. Quite frankly, we live in a society where waiting is seen as a harrowing experience, and one regarded as a great waste of time. Consequently, waiting is viewed as a cause of stress, leading to tension and eventually anger, road rage being a classic example, as is fighting to break out in queues for sales, delayed planes – the list goes on. Where people are told they have to wait, frictions are caused and can lead to all sorts of trouble. However, perhaps more needs to be done to challenge and inform and stress the positivity of waiting.

In the late twentieth century, the negative perception of waiting was challenged, and an advertising slogan was introduced which stated that 'All good things come to those who wait'. It was adopted by the UK advertising campaign for Guinness stout in the 1990s and 2000s and was also used by a US advertising campaign for Heinz ketchup in the 1980s, the manufacture of both products needing to involve long and sometimes complicated processes, before coming to maturity. The idea behind the campaign quite simply involved the belief that if we want quality and perfection there needs to be an element of waiting. It is something we are all aware of and that if we are in a hurry and want to eat, we will go to a fast-food outlet, however, if we want to experience food, we will choose a restaurant. It will mean waiting but we will have more choice, and hopefully have a wider variety of taste, flavour, texture, and we will also have the added benefit of being introduced to different combinations. Consequently, waiting has its benefits, the existence of many of which we may not even be aware of their existence.

Peter Hutchison, writing in The Telegraph (15 Apr 2010), referred to a report published in April's issue of the medical journal Neuron, which stated that a person's decision to delay an instant reward was based on a quick prediction of how successful each outcome would be. He went on to say that experts working in the field of Neuroscience, claimed to have pinpointed a circuit in the brain which tells the human mind to delay seeking immediate satisfaction, thus suggesting that the creators of those popular Guinness adverts, and Heinz adverts, were on to something. The idea of more achievement gained through waiting was a policy adopted by the London Science Museum when their new hands-on activity, LaunchPad, for children aged seven plus, was opened. Although a large area was dedicated to these interactive experiments, in proportion there were fewer activities to the proposed number of children who would be engaged in them. The thinking behind the decision to have the imbalance was that if children had to wait, then they were more likely to engage fully with the activity. In addition to this, while they were waiting, it allowed the children to not only observe what was required of them but also stimulated the mind into problem-solving mode. Waiting has many benefits and should be seen more in a positive light, not that it is a wasting of time but more of a chance to develop patience.

After all, patience is a virtue, a behaviour showing high moral standards, but perhaps one of the most difficult to achieve. Whereas love, joy and peace portrays a Christian's generic mindset, with special emphasis on his relationship with God, patience, or longsuffering as it is referred to in the King James Version and New King James Version. It is similar to kindness, goodness, faithfulness, and self-control in that it contains social virtues relating to our thoughts and actions toward our fellow man and our attitude during trials. Indeed, there is a connection between self-control and patience. In that patience frequently expresses the idea of passivity or resignation in the face of overwhelming difficulties or problems that cannot be changed; quite basically it is acceptance of a very difficult situation. Indeed it is impossible to mention patience in suffering without referring to the character from the Old Testament Job; as Job and patience are synonymous. Indeed a phrase often coined in our language is 'to have the patience of Job'. Thus to have the patience of Job is seen as someone who can endure sufferings and trials with unwavering faith and trust in God.

The story of Job, one of the greatest examples of someone showing great restraint in the face of adversity, is the first poetic book of the Wisdom Books in the Old Testament and is classified as such because the majority of Job is written in parallel lines, which is indicative of poetry. It is a long dialogue poem, with a prose prologue and epilogue, involving Job, his friends and eventually, God. Indeed in the introduction to the book, the Jerusalem Bible states that it is 'the literary masterpiece of the wisdom movement', due to the fact it is regarded by many as God's inspired answer to the issue of suffering in life.

The Book of Job focuses on questions about God's justice and why good people suffer. Job, his wife, and his friends speculate on why he, Job, a good and upright man, should endure horrendous disasters that take away all that he holds dear, including his children, his health, and his property. In ancient Israel, three assumptions were fundamental to the theology of Job and his friends, and they were that God is almighty, perfectly just and that no human is pure in his sight. In the Old Testament, sin and suffering were connected because of the nature of the covenant. It was believed that keeping God's statutes resulted in being blessed, and not keeping them resulted in being cursed (Lev. 26:1-46, Deut. 27:15-26). Therefore, the concluding logic would be that every person's suffering is indicative of the measure of their guilt in the eyes of God. However, the Book of Job challenges this perception as there were people like Job who were moral upright, godly fearing men and who had kept themselves from great transgression, but who nonetheless were made to suffer bitterly.

Initially, when Job learns of the disasters that have befallen him, his words are,

"Naked I came from my mother's womb, naked I shall return.

Yahweh gave, Yahweh has taken back

Blessed be the name of Yahweh" (Job 1:21).

However, after the arrival of his three friends, there were seven days and seven nights where they sat in silence with Job, "They never spoke a word, so sad a sight he made" (Job 2:13). Then Job starts off cursing the day he was born, blaming God for all his misfortunes, pointing out that he has been a good god-fearing man and didn't deserve all the misfortune, as he had done nothing wrong to warrant them. Job speaks of foundational themes every human being contends with, especially in times of suffering. He was totally honest about his feelings right from the onset, both with God and with his friends, but mainly with himself, which allowed him to enter into a meaningful, purposeful dialogue. In consequence, as Job is thinking aloud, being reflective there is a subtle change in his attitude towards his misfortunes. This becomes apparent when he starts conversing with his three friends, and the anger he feels towards God's injustice towards him changes and he begins to defend God.

There are many lessons we can learn from the Book of Job and the first one is about how we deal with and view trials and tribulations. Although Job had no idea why he had to endure all the suffering and loss, all the negative things that were happening to him, he continued to put his trust implicitly in God. "Though He slay me, yet will I trust Him" (Job 13.15). Although he had asked for an answer to why God was punishing him, he never received an answer. But more importantly, he received a deeper understanding of who God is, he came to know the God he served. Sometimes we are not meant to understand the reason for our trials and tribulations, we just need to accept them with child-like faith and trust knowing that all trials and tribulations, can be turned into a powerful learning curve that takes us closer to God. Just because we are Christians does not mean we will not have to face difficult challenges within our life, but it does mean they can help us to grow spiritually if we allow them.

Saint Paul, in his letter to the Romans, makes very clear his awareness of the struggles Christians may face in the world but emphasises the fact that far from threatening our peace they can be used to draw us closer to God. "Rejoice in suffering and it will change your heart" (Romans 5:3, NKJV). The same advice is given in the Jerusalem Bible with a little more explanation, "We can boast about our sufferings. These sufferings bring patience, as we know, and patience brings perseverance, and perseverance brings hope, and this hope is not deceptive, because the love of God has been poured into our hearts by the Holy Spirit which has been given to us (Romans 5:3-6). Sometimes when we suffer in trials, all we can concentrate is on the here and now, how we are being affected. Saint Paul encourages us to adopt a different attitude, to look beyond them and so to become aware that the Lord wants to teach us through them; and to bring trials and tribulations together, both for our good and for His glory.

This theme constantly appears throughout the Bible where we are encouraged to persevere in our trials, with hope and trust as it will be a means of God refining us. James, the brother of the Lord wrote "My brothers, you will always have your trials but, when they come, try to treat them as a happy privilege, you understand that your faith is only put to the test to make you patient, but patience too is to have its practical results so that you will become fully developed, complete with nothing missing" (The Letter of James 1:2–5) and later in the letter, "Happy the man who stands firm when trials come. He has proved himself and will win the prize of life, the crown that the Lord has promised to those who love him" (James 1:12).

Isaiah, Chapter 54, expands on the theme of embracing and enduring trials, however difficult they may be as they are a means of God drawing us closer to Him, and so consequently will, through perseverance, lead to a very beautiful conclusion. "Unhappy creature, storm-tossed, disconsolate, see I will set your stones on carbuncles and your foundations on sapphires, I will make rubies your battlements, your gates crystal, and your entire wall precious stones" (Isaiah 54:11–12). In the Old and New Testament, fire, sea, and storms are used both literally and metaphorically, to help develop a deeper understanding of our relationship with God and God's relationship with us. In the first verse, 'unhappy creature, storm-tossed,' Isaiah paints a picture of chaos and disorder causing turmoil, leaving the person with feelings of unhappiness, synonyms of which are feelings of being: dejected, regretful, depressed, downcast, miserable, downhe arted,

despondent, despairing, wretched, glum, gloomy, doleful, di smal, blue, melancholy, melancholic, low-
spirited, mournful, woeful, and so the list goes on. However, if we look to the Lord and trust him then at the end of the storm we will be transformed. All the rough edges from us will have been removed, leaving behind a beautiful, polished stone. Chaim Bentorah in his book, 'Hebrew Study: Revealing the Heart of God', likens the storm-tossed process of the pebbles to the method used to refine semi-precious stones. They are put in a metal container with water and then the tin is revolved backwards and forwards until the pebbles are smooth and polished. This is what God is doing to us when we face trials, He is polishing us just like gemstones, until all our rough, jagged edges are removed, and we begin to shine.

Isaiah also draws on the metaphorically use of fire and water to explain how God wants to help us during our times of trial. "Do not be afraid for I have redeemed you; I have called you by your name, you are mine. Should you pass through the sea, I will be with you; or through rivers, they will not swallow you up. Should you walk through the fire, you will not be scorched, and the flames will not burn you. For I am Yahweh your God, the Holy One of Israel, your saviour" (Isaiah 43:1–3). When the phrase 'pass-through' is used in the Bible it refers to travelling; moving forward; a journey. Similarly, when rivers are mentioned, it can be literal in that they refer to all kinds of watercourses, including wadis (dried-up desert riverbeds) and permanent rivers but they could also be used symbolically; to refer to things that threaten or overwhelm people and nations, such as invading nations, trials, and tribulations and more importantly the loss of the peace of God.

In the first verse, Isaiah talks about passing through both rivers and seas, which may have a two-fold meaning. Although seas in the Bible can symbolise bodies of water connected with danger death, evil and chaos, Isaiah could also be referring to the miraculous passage of the Israelites through the Red sea, and the river Jordan; and to God's destroying the Egyptians, and the Assyrian, or Babylonian empire, to deliver his people out of slavery and persecution into a land filled with milk and honey. "And so I have resolved to bring you out of Egypt where you are oppressed, into the land of the Canaanites – to a land where milk and honey flow" (Exodus 3:17), milk and honey being a metaphor for all good things. Not only is God promising to deliver us with the words, 'I will', but there is also reassurance in the phrase, the rivers will not, 'swallow you up', a metaphor meaning to fully consume or envelop someone.

If not careful, all our suffering and hardships can envelop us, making us insular and prone to feeling sorry for ourselves, to the point where we become immersed in negativity, filled with despair and despondency. Instead of looking inward, in times of trial we need to look upwards, to heaven, "I lift my eyes to the mountains: where is help to come from? Help comes to me from Yahweh, who made heaven and earth" (Psalm 121:1–2). Indeed, many of the Psalms speak about God's love and protection and how they, the Psalmist, had been protected and delivered, as they journeyed through the trials of life. "Though I pass through a gloomy valley, I fear no harm; beside me, your rod and staff are there to hearten me" (Psalm 23: 4–5). In these verses, the rod is used metaphorically as protection and staff as support. The Talmud teaches the darker the shadow the closer the Lord, and this is exactly what King David, as the Psalmist is implying in Psalm 23.

Not only is God close to us in our trials, but we also learn from Isaiah that, "Should you walk through the fire, you will not be scorched, and the flames will not burn you" (Isaiah 43:2). In this instance, fire is used as a representation of purification or to be illuminating or enlightening; as of the mind. All the misfortunes of Job didn't turn him into a bitter twisted person feeling sorry for himself, instead, through perseverance and dialogue, the trials led him into a new enlightened state of mind; into a more intimate relationship with God, he loved and trusted.

Indeed, one of the many lessons we can learn from Job is that instead of crying out to God and apportioning blame when troubles come, we need, to spend time in silence, in contemplation, reflecting, so that we can learn what it is that God is trying to teach us through our misfortunes. We need to take a more spiritual approach, and this happens in the final part of the book where Job decides to speak directly to God. It is this dialogue with God, that can be described as pure meditation, a deep spiritual meeting between Job's spirit and God's which allows not only healing to occur but ultimately allows Job to come to an understanding of, and to acknowledge, his deep dependence on God.

Like Job, we need to learn to meditate, to make time to sit in silence. The English word for meditation is derived from the Latin *'meditation'*, the verb *'meditari'*, meaning 'to think, contemplate, devise or ponder'. It has a similar meaning in the Old French from the word *'meditacion'*, which means thought, reflection or to study. The importance of Meditation, Christian meditation, like silence cannot be underestimated; it is essential for growth in our spiritual life. We are spiritual beings yet, so often, it is our physical needs that we attend to, and the spiritual is ignored. Like Job, we need to learn how to sit in silence and allow the Holy Spirit to speak to us, to enter into dialogue with God. According to the Benedictine monk, and a Director of the World Community for Christian Meditation, Lawrence Freeman, "Meditation is simple, being simple means being ourselves. It means passing beyond self-consciousness, self-analysis, and self-rejection. Meditation is a universal spiritual practise that guides us into this state of prayer, into the prayer of Christ. It brings us to silence, stillness and simplicity by a means that is itself silent, still and simple" (www.christianmeditation.org.uk).

In Psalm 46, the Psalmist calls us to come before the Lord in stillness, silence, and simplicity, "Be still and know that I am God" (Psalm 46:10). As a Christian, when we meditate, we come into spiritual communion with God. Unlike eastern meditation, which advocates emptying the mind, Christian meditation calls on us to open our minds to receive God's revelations and His truths. To achieve a stillness, there needs to be a detachment from the world and an attachment to God. It is not a coincidence that the first letter of the Hebrew alphabet is the Aleph, a silent letter, and a reminder that we need to be silent before God. It signifies that everything we achieve in our life has its beginning in stillness and silence. According to Chaim Bentorah in his book, 'Learning God's love language: a guide to Personal Hebrew study', "Silence is nothing and yet it is everything."

Consequently, it was through meditation that Job had come to acknowledge his dependence on God, through his inner reflections, his fortunes began to change. However, it was only when he prayed for his friends that his fortunes were restored. "Yahweh restored Job's fortunes" (because he had prayed for his friends, who had been there for him in his hour of need but though well-meaning their advice had been misguiding). "More than that, Yahweh gave Job double what he had before" (Job 42:10–11). Although Job's friends did come to him and empathised with him in his troubles, even sitting in silence with him for seven days, when they then broke their silence, they gave lengthy speeches, mostly inaccurate, proclaiming that Job must have offended God and therefore must repent. They meant well but as the saying goes, 'the road to hell is paved with good intentions'. After all, they had given their time and did all to help their friend when he needed companionship, even going that little bit further. They were true friends in every sense of the word. Indeed the fourth letter of the Hebrew alphabet, the Gimmel has a primary meaning of loving kindness but the shadow of the Gimmel warns about overzealousness when trying to do good deeds, which can result in harm. In this case, these really good friends of Job ended up doing more damage than good, in trying to be helpful, through giving him inexperienced spiritual advice. They were trying to impose their limited understanding of God, and God's provision for us, onto Job.

A vital lesson that all of us must learn in order to please God and to begin emerging from a trial is that we need to show mercy and forgiveness. Job's friends were, and are still to this day, referred to as miserable comforters, hence the phrase Job's comforter being used to apply to someone more of a hindrance than a help in times of trials. Yet the turning point occurred when Job began to emerge from his great adversity; and blessed them; not cursed them, but *blessed them*. "And the LORD restored Job's losses when he prayed for his friends" (42:10).

Job came to know God deeply, not simply to know about Him. He became a far more humble and compassionate man as a result of what he went through. Growth is not easy, but instead of wanting vindication for those who we feel have put stumbling blocks in our way, especially in a time of trial, we can see them as challenges for us to help us grow in our spiritual life. In doing so, we can be merciful towards them and forgive their shortcomings. Learning this lesson was instrumental in helping Job emerge out of the dark shadows of life and into the sunlight once again.

And to continue to live in this sunlight, we should not become anxious or worry about the future. We need to learn to live in the present trusting in God to provide all our needs. Jesus reminded us of this fact both in Luke's gospel and the same verses that appear in Matthew's gospel (12:25-34), when he told his disciples, not to worry about the two essential requirements for the body. "That is why I am telling you not to worry about your life and what you are to eat, nor about your body and how you are to cloth it. For life means more than food, and the body more than clothing" (Luke 12: 22-23). "But you must not set your heart on things to eat and things to drink; nor must you worry. It is the pagans of this world who set their hearts on all these things. Your Father well knows but he still knew that life is more than food and the body more than clothing, the spiritual is you need them. No; set your hearts on the kingdom, and these other things will be given to you as well. There is no need to be afraid, little flock, for it has pleased your father to give you the kingdom" (Luke 12:28–32).

We need to take these words from Jesus to our hearts and, in addition, to learn from Job the importance of patience in our spiritual life. If we are to grow spiritually then we need to sit patiently waiting for the lord to act; to sit and allow the Holy Spirit to speak to us. When we allow this to happen we can rise above our ego, our self-consciousness, into sincerity, a willingness to surrender to the promptings of the Holy Spirit and to be obedient to His voice. It is in the silence that we can

67

let go of our ego, our self-seeking, our analytical nature and stand empty in the presence of God allowing Him to fill us with His words, His Spirit of love. He will communicate with us joining His heart to our heart, our Spirit joined to His Holy Spirit. In our nothingness are His help and protection. He will minister to us in kindness and love.

Chapter Four
Kindness

"The Lord is kind and full of compassion" (Psalm 144).

Kindness, the quality of being friendly, generous, and considerate, is quite simply a personal quality that enables an individual to be sensitive and to show empathy to others, thus it is a way of showing love. It is indicative of having a sympathetic, affectionate, warm-hearted, considerate nature. No matter how small the act of kindness may be, it can still have an impact on another person's life. According to Amelia Earhart (PassItOn.com), "A single act of kindness throws out roots in all directions, and the roots spring up and make new trees", and in the words of Mark Twain, "Kindness is a language which the deaf can hear and the blind can see" (www.brainyquote.com). However, to think of kindness as being just simple little acts that help make others' lives brighter is to misunderstand the complexity of the act.

In the same category as joy and patience, kindness is a virtue and thus, as stated earlier, is a behaviour marked by moral principles, and a concern and consideration of others. However, it is important to remember that for kindness to become a virtue, it should not be just a single act, a one-off, but rather it has to be a consistent trait that is displayed over time and just as importantly, important is an act of kindness which should not be falsely, or to receive something in return. Kindness, unlike patience, is possibly one of the easiest virtues to develop, and yet one that can have far-reaching effects both in our own lives and the lives of others. Often one of the most tear-inducing stories we hear is that of the kindness of complete strangers to those in need. Indeed when we stop pampering our egos and start looking around us with the eyes of Jesus we can see many people who need an act of kindness. The Jewish sages teach that kindness is rooted in the heart and from the heart, it flows. Therefore, as it is a matter of the heart; it's linked to that first fruit of the Spirit, love. Saint Basil paints a beautiful analogy when describing acts of kindness, "A tree is known by its fruit; a man by his deeds. A good deed is never lost; he who sows courtesy reaps friendship, and he who plants kindness gathers love" (www.goodreads.com).

The act of kindness needs to come straight from the heart, with empathy being the driving force. Empathy, the ability to understand and share the feelings of another, by imagining what it would be like to be in their situation should not be confused with sympathy, the 'feelings of pity and sorrow for someone else's misfortune'. When confusion arises between these two emotions acts of kindness may also be affected. If we act because we are feeling sorry for the person, we may do more damage than good, as we are trying to change the situation to make us feel better, not the other person, so our actions could be based on selfish reasons and consequently be detrimental, having a negative impact. Perhaps that is why the shadow of the third letter of the Hebrew alphabet, the

Gimmel's negative aspect warns us about being overzealous in trying to show loving kindness.

There are other 'hidden' dangers associated with showing kindness. In Matthew's Gospel, Jesus warns us, "Be careful not to parade your good deeds before men to attract their notice; by doing this you will lose all reward from your Father in heaven. So when you give alms do not have it trumpeted before you; this is what hypocrites do in the synagogues, and in the street, to win men's admiration" (Matthew 6:3). Thus according to Jesus, our good deeds must not be done to impress, to gain 'respect' from others, and consequently, our motives for giving alms should be pure or they could be construed as being selfish, using others suffering to advance our standing within the community. Instead, Jesus was very clear on what we should do, "But when you give alms your left hand must not know what your right hand is doing; your almsgiving must be in secret, and your Father who sees all that is done in secret will reward you" (Matthew 6:4).

By speaking in this way to the Jewish people, Jesus was reinforcing the message of the Hebrew letter the Gimmel; both the positive and the negative aspects as the main focus or one of the primary meanings of the Gimmel is as to show loving kindness, to those around us. The letter is shaped like that of a man in motion, running to find those who are poorer than he is, so he can provide nourishment for them. However, it is not a one-off action, but a reminder that one needs to grow to bestow kindness and nourishment to his neighbour. It needs to become a way of life, not only developing the generosity of the spirit but also developing an awareness of those who are in need. However, the shadow of the Gimmel is the danger of overzealousness in trying to show loving kindness and thus resulting in harm. Therefore there is a need to be thoughtful and skilful when we perform acts of kindness for others.

The Gimmel also represents the kindness of God, His eternal benevolence and is referred to in the Psalms more than eighty times. It was not only the Psalmist who referred to God's loving-kindness but Nehemiah attributed God's mercy and kindness to not abandoning the Israelites when they rebelled and turned against him, on their journey to the Promised Land. "They refused to listen And did not remember Your wondrous deeds which You had performed among them; So they became stubborn and appointed a leader to return to their slavery in, Egypt But You are a God of forgiveness, Gracious and compassionate, Slow to anger and abounding in lovingkindness; And You did not forsake them" (Nehemiah 9:17).

Nehemiah, who was instrumental in the rebuilding and reestablishment of Jerusalem in the fifth century B.C. following the Babylonian exile was no stranger to acting in love and kindness through empathy. His story appears in the Books of Ezra and Nehemiah, following Chronicles. Although appearing now as two separate works in the English Bibles, they were, before the sixteenth century, one book and dealt with the 'Return to Zion', following the end of the 'Babylonian captivity'. Both men worked together to restore the city of Jerusalem and rededicate its people to God. Nehemiah served as the king's cupbearer (Nehemiah 1:11) a job involving guarding against poison in the king's cup and thus his confidential relations with the king often gave him a position of great influence.

The Book opens with the account of Nehemiah receiving a report about Jerusalem's distress: that its walls are broken, and its gates are on fire. "'Those who escaped from captivity,' they replied, who are back there in the province, are in great trouble and humiliation; the walls of Jerusalem are in ruins" (Nehemiah 1:3). Nehemiah's response on hearing this was to weep for his people and cry out to God for mercy. "On hearing this I sank down and wept; for several days I mourned, fasting and praying before the God of heaven" (Nehemiah 1:4).

Nehemiah's empathy led him to act for his people. He acquired the king's permission to return to Jerusalem and rebuild the city and its fortifications. Although he returned as its provincial governor, he didn't take advantage of his position and the benefits that had allowed him due to his office, as he felt there was already such a great burden on the people of his province (Nehemiah 5:14–19). In addition to this, he also made the other nobles and officials forgive all outstanding debts and ordered them to return all land and money that had been taken as taxes so the people would be able to feed themselves and their families. Thus he was and is a great example of how to lead effectively, without abusing the power that comes with the elevated position. Put quite simply, he led with empathy and power, a winning combination, and so under Nehemiah's leadership, the Jews withstood opposition and came together to accomplish their goal. They rebuilt the gates and walls of the temple in fifty-two days. In this account not only was the kindness the bonding force between Nehemiah and the Jewish people but it also allowed the Chosen people to experience the loving-kindness of God.

Another story of empathy led to a great sacrificial act of kindness which in turn led to a deepening relationship between God and His people, involving one of the ancestors of Jesus. It occurred in the Old Testament, in the Book of Ruth and told the story of Ruth a Moabite princess, who became the great-grandmother of King David. The central themes of the book of Ruth are trust, loyalty, kindness, and God's faithfulness. According to the Midrash (an ancient commentary on part of the Hebrew Scriptures, attached to the biblical text), the book of Ruth was written to teach how great the reward is to those who do deeds of kindness, as not only they prosper but so do those around them. It is a win-win situation, and it is also a reminder that everything we do affects not only our own lives but touches other lives, too.

The book of Ruth is the story about a normal Israelite family, Elimelech, his wife Naomi, and their two sons, Mahlon, and Chilion. Due to a famine in the land, the family had to leave Bethlehem to go live in Moab (Ruth 1:1–2). While there Elimelech dies and his sons Mahlon and Chilion marry. Namoni inherits two daughters-in-law, Orpah and Ruth but ten years later, her sons also die. On hearing that God has provided food in Bethlehem, Naomi desolate with the loss of her sons and their provision for her decides to return home. Her daughters-in-law accompany her at first. However, after urging both of them to go back to their people, Orpah leaves, but Ruth, motivated by her love for her mother-in-law, refuses to abandon her. This refusal to abandon her mother-in-law was a great act of kindness, inspired by empathy.

She "clung to her, proclaiming "wherever you go I will go, wherever you live I will live, your people will be my people, and your God, my God" (Ruth 1:16–17). In uttering these words Ruth, a Moabite princess gave up the privileges that belonged to her in her own country and accepted a life of poverty.

On their return to Bethlehem, they were very poor, and Ruth was reduced to 'gleaning' in the fields, during the harvest. Gleaning was the custom of following the men harvesting the crop and picking up the remains of grain which were left behind. This custom was used primarily for the poor, who had little or no means of supporting themselves. These disenfranchised people were often the widows and the elderly who had lost their husbands or relatives due to death or abandonment and had no other way to survive. The practice of gleaning stemmed from a law of God, found in Leviticus 19: 9, "When you gather the harvest of your land, you are not to harvest to the very end of the field. You are not to gather the gleanings of your harvest." The reason for this is further expounded in Leviticus 23:22), "When you gather in your country, you are not to harvest to the very end of your field, and you are not to gather the gleanings of the harvest. You are to leave them for the poor and the stranger." Even today, in certain parts of Syria, this custom still prevails, where these deeds of kindness are seen just as a way of life, and as such the owners of the fields are never expected to be repaid.

Ruth's kindness to Naomi, however, was inadvertently repaid to her, by Boaz the owner of the barley field, where she was working. Boaz was not only a wealthy landowner of Bethlehem in Judea, but he was also a kinsman of Elimelech, Naomi's late husband. Boaz told Ruth that she could continue to glean from his fields as needed and even take some of the water the men had drawn. He added that he had also given orders to the men not to touch her. When Ruth asked why he was doing this for her, he told her it was because of all she had done for Naomi. Thus out of compassion and obedience to the law, he allowed Ruth to glean but in addition to this, he had ordered his workers not only to look out for her but also to purposely leave extra grains for her. In doing so, Boaz displayed what is in Hebrew called 'hesed', a merciful, compassionate, grace-filled loving kindness. Boaz and Ruth fell in love, married, and produce a son, Obed, the father of Jesse, who became the father of David.

Thus the story of Ruth is a good example of how kindness softens hearts, lifts spirits and moulds relationships. However, it is not only the Old Testament where there are examples of kindness. There are many examples in the New Testament of Jesus acting in a merciful, compassionate way, and in which lives were touched very powerfully. The definition of compassion, which is more related to empathy than sympathy, in that it is a feeling of deep sympathy and sorrow for another who is hurting, in pain, or has misfortune and is accompanied by a strong desire to help those suffering. The Bible defines the meaning of compassion in several ways. We are to "speak up for those who cannot speak for themselves; defend the rights of the poor and needy" (Proverbs 31:8–9, NIV). Jesus put it more simply when He said, "So always treat others as you would like them to treat you; that is the meaning of the Law and the Prophets" (Matthew 7:12). Throughout the ministry of Jesus, he often spoke on this theme, but more importantly, He acted on it with genuine compassion, which in return led to remarkable healings and miracles. Indeed, in the Bible Jesus is the greatest example of someone whose kind actions are grounded in true compassion.

In the New Testament, the Evangelists, Mark, Matthew, and Luke consistently use the word compassion to refer to the heart of the gospel: God's response to human suffering. Mark captures the essence of the matter when he introduces his two stories of the miracles of the feeding the multitude, by referring to Jesus' compassion. "And he had compassion on them" (Mark 6:34). The first miracle, 'Feeding of the 5,000' or as it is more commonly known as, 'The miracles of the five loaves and two fishes', is reported by all four Evangelists, Matthew (14:13–21); Mark (6:31–44); Luke (9:12–17); John (6:1–14). It takes place after Jesus had been told of the death of John the Baptist. Although Mark and Luke make references to the miracle happening after the disciples had returned from their evangelistic mission triumphant but exhausted, thus having a reason for Jesus showing them compassion, leading them to a quiet place to rest, Matthew takes a different stand. He links with the death of John the Baptist being the reason that Jesus had requested them to go off by themselves, "When Jesus received this news he withdrew by boat to a lonely place where they could be by themselves (Matthew 14:13). Thus according to Matthew, Jesus was grieving for John and hence the need to withdraw to a 'lonely' place. However, before Jesus could even step on dry ground, "The people heard of this and leaving the towns, went after him on foot. So as he stepped ashore he saw a large crowd" (Matthew 12:14).

Normally, a grieving process involves elements of feeling sorry for ourselves, our loss and consequently we tend to turn inward, to be aware of our needs, and to have an expectation for our needs, our sorrows to be addressed, to be catered to, but this is not the case with Jesus. Even though he was grieving over the death of John, his cousin, Jesus was looking outward, not inward, and so was aware of the suffering that surrounded him, which in turn allowed Him to act with loving-kindness, "He had compassion on them and healed their sick" (Matthew 14:14) (NIV). There are other examples in Matthew's gospel of Jesus showing compassion and healing the sick, such as the widow at Nain.

"As he approached the town gate, a dead person was being carried out – the only son of his mother, and she was a widow. And a large crowd from the town was with her. When the Lord saw her, his heart went out to her and he said, 'Don't cry.' Then he went up and touched the bier they were carrying him on, and the bearers stood still. He said, 'Young man, I say to you, get up!' The dead man sat up and began to talk, and Jesus gave him back to his mother" (Luke 7:12–16, NIV). The similarity between this story and the story of Ruth is that both Naomi and this woman had lost both a husband and a son, their sole providers. They were left destitute! In this story, however, it is Jesus who transforms the hopeless situation. By gently ordering the mother not to cry, He was reassuring her that He was there in the midst of her suffering. Ignoring the fact that touching a dead body would make him religiously unclean, Jesus stopped the funeral procession, touched the young man, and commanded him to get up.

There are other examples of Jesus using touch to reach out to the untouchables, those in society who normally would be shunned. In Matthew's gospel, there is the story of a leper who approached Jesus, bowed low and said, "Sir, if you want to, you can cure me" (Matthew 8:2). It is not hard to imagine Jesus smiling at the leper, stretching out and touching him, while saying with an empathic tone of voice, "Of course I want to! Be cured!" And his leprosy was cured at once (Matthew 8:3–4). Again lepers were untouchable and the fact that Jesus touched a leper was a powerful demonstration of His willingness to ignore social taboo and be ruled instead by a loving concern for the suffering individual.

Jesus also used touch to heal the blind beggars while He and the disciples were leaving Jericho, however, in this healing, there is a subtle difference. The men had heard the commotion and learnt that it was because Jesus was passing so they called out to Him, "Lord, have pity on us, son of David" (Matthew 20:31). Although the crowd tried to silence them, they called even louder and by addressing Jesus as Son of David, they were acknowledging that in their blind state they recognised that he was the Messiah, the Chosen One. Instead of going to them, however, Jesus *called* them to *come* to Him, and then asked the question, "What do you want me to do for you?" Although it may have seemed obvious what the men wanted, i.e. their sight back, Jesus, didn't heal them immediately, 'out of pity'. He wasn't overzealous in showing them kindness! Instead, he challenged them. After all, begging was a way of life and once they could see again, their way of life would be greatly changed, and they would have to fend for themselves instead of relying on others. Thus when they answered, "Lord let us have our sight back," Jesus had compassion on them and touched their eyes. Immediately, they received their sight and followed him (Matthew 20: 33-34). When we call out for Jesus to pity us, we need to listen to the question Jesus will ask of us. It is so easy to get carried away with the moment or be influenced by those around us; in this case, the crowd telling the blind men to be quiet, when we call out to Jesus to set us free from the darkness and restore our sight so we will be able to 'see', we do need to be aware of what it means, to follow Jesus in the light, to follow a completely different path.

As Jesus demonstrated throughout His ministry, kindness is no small thing and is greatly beneficial to all. Indeed when we learn to show kindness in our lives, marvellous fruits will occur not only for us but for others too. "He who pursues virtue and kindness shall find life and honour too" (Proverbs 21:21). However, not only do we gain from showing kindness, but we also imitate God's kindness, especially when we love our enemies. Jesus said, "Love your enemies, and do good, and lend, expecting nothing in return, and your reward will be great, and you will be sons of the Most High, for he is kind to the ungrateful and the evil" (Luke 6:35). How wonderful, our kindness reflects the heart of God, our Father!

According to a belief I have heard from a Shetlander, when we die and go to the pearly gates, the first five people we meet will be ones we don't recognise. They are there, however, because when we were on our journey through life their little act of kindness, unbeknown to us, helped us grow and consequently come closer to God. Acts of kindness can never be underestimated!

Chapter Five
Goodness

"I remain confident of this: I will see the goodness of the Lord in the land of the living" (Psalm 27:13).

Goodness follows kindness in the fruits of the Spirit and just as a vine grows and intertwines so it is with the fruits of the Spirit, all of them are linked. Goodness, which is also a virtue, is connected to kindness, indeed some dictionaries define the word as being, kind, generous and honest, thereby making this link, but with an additional aspect, that of truthfulness. However, this definition is limited as goodness encompasses so much more than that which appears to have got lost in translation, through the ages.

Although the word goodness is rarely used today, unless under exceptional circumstances, or to relate to health benefits, there are related phrases that have crept into our language: 'Goodness!' – used to make a statement more forceful; 'My Goodness! – to show surprise; 'Out of the goodness of her heart' – used to describe an act of personal generosity done without expectation of a reward or acknowledgement, and as a euphemism for God, 'Thank Goodness!' Indeed, there is a belief that the English word for 'good' originated from the word 'god'. Certainly, the closest idiom to that of the virtue of goodness is 'out of the goodness of her heart', which gives us more of an understanding of the quality involved in the act. However, before exploring the quality of goodness, perhaps the best way to come to a deeper understanding of the word is, to begin with, its root word, 'good'.

Similarly to love, the word good is used in our language today, is overused and is considered more akin to the word 'nice', meaning a little better than mediocre. It is also relative so that what is perceived as being good to one person may not be shared with another. It is actually our overuse of the word that has restricted the meaning because according to the dictionary the word good which is an adjective, has meanings that include having the required qualities; of a high standard, and possessing or displaying moral virtue (Google Dictionaries). Its synonyms are many and include qualities of being virtuous, righteous, moral, correct, ethical, principled, law-abiding, and honest. Whereas the antonyms for good are bad, evil, sinful, immoral, inadequate, mean, rotten, unreliable, vile, unsuitable, and wicked. Therefore, the opposite of good is often compared to bad or more importantly evil.

It would appear that in the light of these defining qualities, the important uses of the word good/goodness have to do with moral qualities; the principles of right and wrong behaviour; or manifesting high principles for proper conduct. It is important to note that morals relate to standards of good behaviour, fairness, honesty, and principles or what each person believes in, rather than to laws. Consequently, according to the Easton Bible Dictionary, "Goodness in man is not a mere passive quality, but the deliberate preference of right to wrong, the firm and persistent resistance of all moral evil, and the choosing and following of all moral good," while the Cambridge Academic Content Dictionary defines it more simply as "The quality of being morally right and admirable" (Cambridge University Press). Morals are therefore arbitrary as they pertain to the standards that people hold, but because they are linked to fairness, honesty, principles, virtue, etc. They do have a benchmark, a beginning from where to develop. In 'Heart of Darkness', the author Joseph Conrad sees the inner evil as a human's struggle with their morals, and their battle with their hidden evil. A simple explanation of this inner struggle appeared recently on Facebook. It tells the story told of an Indigenous American Chief who had just converted to Christianity. When asked what it was like to be a Christian, he pondered and then replied, "Well, each day it is like I have two dogs fighting within me, one good and one bad." The interviewer immediately asked, "And which one wins?" The quick response was, "Ah, the one I feed the most." And so it is with us, this constant struggle between good and evil, the yin and the yan, the contrary forces that have existed since creation, that occur within us, and of course, the one we indulge in, give more time and attention to will be the one who will reign in our lives.

Genesis, the first book of the Bible, tells the story of creation, and begins with the words, "In the beginning, God created the heavens and the earth" (Genesis 1:1). Creation deals with bringing order out of chaos, through separation. The process starts with light being separated from the dark, the night and day; then continues with the sky and sea; land and vegetation; stars, sun, moon; sea creatures and birds; and finally animals and humans, and at each stage, "God saw that it was good." The word 'good' in Hebrew is *tov* which is to be in harmony with someone or something and when used in Genesis, means it was in harmony with God, with the creator. Tov begins with the Hebrew letter Tet, which has positive connotations of goodness. However, there is also a certain duality associated with this Hebrew letter. Thus, while it is the first letter in the Hebrew word for 'purity', it is also the first letter in the Hebrew word for 'impurity'. As the first letter in the word for 'good' which is used to describe God's reaction to the creation of light; the separation between the light and the darkness, it is also connecting the idea of duality, the light and dark, good, and bad etc.

At the close of Chapter 2, in Genesis, there is no sign of this duality as there is a world where everything is 'very good', in complete harmony with God; no pain, no suffering, no disharmony, no suffering, or death. In the case of humanity, we read that "God created mankind in the image of himself; in the image of God he created him; male and female he created them" (Genesis 1:27). Thus in the beginning all, man, and woman, were created good, were in perfect harmony with God. There was no dissension, no division. However, this was about to change when all the positivity was infiltrated by negativity; good was contaminated by bad, or to give it an overall term evil; which was introduced into the world. The introduction of evil begins in the story of Adam and Eve through their disobedience and greed and continues to be a central theme running through the bible; the ongoing conflict between good and evil.

Just as the story of creation is hotly contested in our world today so also is the story of Adam and Eve. However, to take them as factual is missing a point. Genesis, which deals with all the beginning of life on earth is meant to inform or give a message of who God is, how and why he acts and how he deals with mankind. What is important is not how the word was created, that is the job of a scientist, and quite surprisingly their findings may not always be in conflict with the biblical account, as in the case of the Big Bang Theory which begins with a burst of light followed by order replacing chaos, quite similar to the story of creation as it appears in Genesis.

Indeed, we can come to understand many things in our natural world, but there are many things in the spiritual world we will never understand. The Torah teaches that we must not attempt to try to understand as they are beyond our realm of comprehension. Thus science can be useful and help us to become aware of the infinite power of a creator, but it cannot explain God's purpose for creation, and we need to look elsewhere for a reason. It occurs in Genesis, and it is the story of Adam and Eve that gives an explanation of why we are created.

The story of Adam and Eve begins in the Garden of Eden describing the idyllic existence of the first human couple to be created. However, their creation was different from the plants and animals because, "God fashioned man of dust from soil. Then he breathed into his nostrils a breath of life, and thus man became a living being" (Genesis 2:7). Man was created with the breath of God, His Spirit. With this breath which brought life also came a free will, an allowance to make choices which is apparent in the first words God spoke to man, "You may eat indeed of all the trees in the garden. Nevertheless of the tree of the knowledge of good and evil you are not to eat, for on the day you eat from it, you will surely die" (Genesis 2; 16–18). It is worth noting that there are many versions of the Bible which use the term the Tree of Knowledge. In Jewish tradition, the Tree of Knowledge and the eating of its fruit represents the beginning of the mixture of good and evil together.

There is an argument that according to the Bible, God is good, and that all He created was good therefore, 'evil' does not and cannot exist in the physical or spiritual reality that God created (allaboutgod.com). The analogy supporting this statement uses the idea of light and darkness; darkness being the absence of light. The existence of Light can not only be proven but can be measured and artificially created. Darkness, however, does not exist. Dark is what occurs when there is no light; the absence of light. Consequently, the absence of 'good' things always creates 'bad' things. Saint Augustine of Hippo, to a certain extent supported this idea when he stated that the fruits of the Tree of knowledge were not evil by themselves, because everything that God created, 'was good' (Gen 1:12). However, it was the disobedience of Adam and Eve, who had been told by God not to eat of the tree (Gen 2:17), that caused chaos and disorder in the creation story, and consequently, humanity inherited sin and guilt from their disobedience, the first sin, or as it is known original sin.

Sin, the separation of God and man, or man's disobedience to the will of God, starts with Adam and Eve and is still very evident in the world today, and just as in our world today the tempter is often seen as the woman. Initially, the disobedience was attributed to Eve, "The woman saw that the tree was good to eat and pleasing to the eye and that it was desirable for the knowledge that it could give. So she took some of the fruit and ate it. She gave some also to her husband who was with her, and he ate it." Three reasons are given for

Eve's giving in to temptation. It was her greed, 'looked good to eat', 'pleasing to the eye', seduced by beauty; and desire for the knowledge of good and evil, wisdom which ultimately leads to independence from God, whereas true wisdom begins with the fear of the Lord, (Proverbs 1:7) or growing in the knowledge of God so we don't offend or hurt Him. St. Paul states that 'knowledge gives self-importance' (1 Corinthians 8:1): and self-importance is a form of pride; which is regarded as the first sin. Throughout scripture, the essence of sin is to put human judgement above divine command, and this begins in the Garden of Eden.

After they had eaten from the tree, God called to them, "Where are you?" Chaim Bentorah in his book, 'A Hebrew Teacher Reveals the Heart of God', queries the translation used as the original Hebrew word used in this text was Ayaka. And although Ayaka can mean an interrogation, it can also be used as a lamentation or a cry of grief and mourning. It can be an expression of grief, which in this instance would make more sense, than an all-knowing god, having to ask Adam and Eve where they were. Chaim further suggests that as we are created in God's image, then we have a heart like His, a heart that can be broken, and this is what happened in the garden. The sin that broke God's heart was that Adam and Eve turned away from Him. "The man and the woman heard the sound of Yahweh God walking in the garden in the cool of the day and hid from Yahweh God among the trees of the garden" (Genesis 3: 8–9). They were not hiding from God, but from the presence of God, as they had deliberately chosen to turn their back on Him. It was their guilt that caused the separation.

When they did speak to God, Adam refused to take responsibility for his transgression. "The man replied, 'It was the woman you put with me'" (Genesis 3:12). In other words, 'sorry God but it's your fault if you hadn't put me with that woman you and I wouldn't be having this problem'. Then he continues using a phrase every teacher and everyone in authority has come across time and time again, "She gave me the fruit" (Genesis 3:13). In other words, blame her she made me do it. I was forced to disobey you because she coerced me into eating! However this is not quite the story that Genesis teaches, "So she took some of its fruit and ate it. She gave some also to her husband who was with her, and he ate it" (Genesis 3: 6–7). Adam was actually a willing partner in crime but refused to accept the truth and instead turned his back on God, venturing down the road on unrepentance. He didn't accept that he had been fooled, had given in to temptation. Something that is still happening in our world today, our refusal to accept responsibility for our actions, our choices, when we err and give in to temptation; when we try to blame others, even God for our wrongdoing.

James, in his letters, is quite clear about this issue and warns us about our reaction to sin and temptation. "Never, when you have been tempted, say, God sent the temptation; God cannot be tempted to do anything wrong, and he does not tempt anybody. Everyone who is tempted is attracted and tempted by his own wrong desire. Then the desire conceives and gives birth to sin, and when sin is fully grown, it too has a child, and the child is dead" (The Letter of James 1:13–15). And in John's letter, he expands on this theme, "The love of the Father cannot be in any man who loves the world, because nothing the world has to offer – the sensual body, the lustful eye, pride in possessions – could ever come from the Father but only from the world" (1 John 2:15-16). And Paul in his letter to the Romans guides us with his words, "Do not be overcome by evil but overcome evil with good" (Romans 12:9). This is exactly what Jesus taught, in what many consider as probably the most difficult teaching of Jesus, in all of the Gospels: "You have earnt how it was said: You must love your enemies and pray for those who persecute you. But I say this to you: love your enemy, do good to those who hurt you, return good for evil." Jesus went on to explain why, "in this way, you will be sons of the Father in heaven, for he causes his sun to rise on bad men as well as good, and rain to fall on honest men alike" (Matthew 5: 43–46). Jesus was telling us in all situations we have to return good for evil and our decisions for not doing so, are not to be made on judgemental factors. God made all of us, and he loves us regardless of how we respond to that love. In Isaiah, the same sentiment is expressed, but with more emphasis being placed on the fact that we are to trust God, do the right thing, and not retaliate in hatred when faced with evil.

"Should anyone attack you that will not be my doing, and whoever attacks you, for your sake will fall. It was who created the smith who blows on the coal fire and from it takes the weapons to work on. But I also created the destroyer who renders them useless. Not a weapon forged against you will succeed" (Isaiah 54: 15–17). Later in verse 55, Isaiah encourages us to, "Seek Yahweh while he is still to be found, call to him while he is still near. Let the wicked man abandon his way, (note the decision to turn away from evil is an individual choice and first, we must seek God, call to him and then turn our back on evil), the evil man his thoughts." Also worth noting is the fact that our feelings give birth to our thoughts, which then are turned into action, so before we resort to evil deeds, we need to confront our thoughts and, "Turn back to Yahweh who will take pity on (us) him, to our God who is rich in forgiving; for my thoughts are not your thoughts, my ways, not your ways – it is Yahweh who speaks. Yes, the heavens are as high above earth as my ways are above your thoughts" (Isaiah 55: 6–9). Thus when we are dealing with the issue of good versus evil we need to take on a completely different mindset. This is a theme Jesus demonstrated often in his ministry, from his words, especially the Sermon on the Mount also known as the Beatitudes, and especially in his actions.

In Luke's gospel (Chapter 6: 6–16), there is the story of Jesus in the synagogue teaching. Among the people gathered was a man with a withered hand. Not only being aware that the Pharisees were watching him see what he would do, but more importantly, knowing their thoughts, Jesus didn't bow down to pressure by ignoring him, but instead looked directly at the man and said, "Stand up" (6:8). An imperative command, and one which we also need to respond to when faced with a moral dilemma. We need to have the courage to stand up for what is right, not ignore the issue, or look the other way. Jesus confronted the challenge straight on and directed the man to, "Come out into the middle" (6:8). The problem wasn't being swept under the carpet but being made clear. Then Jesus confronted the Pharisees, indirectly holding a mirror up to their conscience, and posed a searching question, " I put it to you is it against the law on the Sabbath to do good, or to do evil; to save life or destroy it" (6:9). A simple question, but then again the questions Jesus asked were never simple or straightforward, they were designed to illuminate what is in the heart, and in this case challenged the perception of man-made laws, the Jewish laws, when they came into conflict with performing acts of mercy.

In the Old Testament where the heart is considered the very basis of character, including mind and will, Jeremiah also deals with what is in our hearts, "The heart is more devious than any other thing, perverse too, who can pierce its secrets?" (Jeremiah 17:9). Since time began, there has been a common mistake among mankind to think their hearts a great deal better than they really are, and this verse from Jeremiah warns against it. We do need to be aware that the heart of man, in his corrupt and fallen state, is false and deceitful above all things; deceitful in masquerading the true reasons for our actions; with respect to sin; a false notion of pleasure; a mere illusion and a dream. It promises happiness through richness, possessions, or job promotion which causes us to pursue wrong directions, wrong courses. Through promoting our pleasures and giving way to our own emotions for selfish reasons there is a danger of the loss of the soul. According to Gill's 'Exposition of the Entire Bible' (Bible Hub), "It (the heart) promises honour and preferment in the world, but promotes him to shame; it promises him liberty, but brings him into bondage; it promises him impunity, peace, and security when sudden destruction comes: it deceives him in point of knowledge; it persuades him that he is a very knowing person when he is blind and ignorant, and knows nothing but perhaps the greatest deception of all is the fact that we believe we have a pure heart, filled with love and goodness."

After all, we do good acts and convince ourselves we are doing them for the glory of God, and not for our glory. We love, but only those that love us. Those we don't love are the ones we have judged to be sinful, evil or those who don't see this wonderful human we are but challenge our motives, our perceptions of ourselves. Jeremiah continues, "I Yahweh search the heart" (Jeremiah 17). Thus, the only one to know what is truly in our hearts is God. He knows our hearts, intimately, every inward part of it; every room and corner in it. Knowing the heart also means He knows the thoughts of it; all its intents, purposes, designs, contrivances, and imaginations; all the secret motions of it, and of course the wickedness that exists within it. So, although the heart is deceitful for us, it cannot deceive God, he sees and knows the heart, He knows us. Thus when Luke states, "But he (Jesus) knew their thoughts" (Luke 6:8), he was giving an indication of the true nature of Jesus because He knew what was in the hearts of the Pharisees; He was able to discern their hearts, it was a revelation that he was more than a mere man, more than a prophet, but was truly the Son of God. "It is I who search heart and loins and give each one of you what your behaviour deserves" (Revelations 2:23). Jesus not only knew what was in men's hearts but used an analogy of fruit trees to teach us how we can come to know what is in our hearts, "There is no sound tree that produces rotten fruit, nor again a rotten tree that produces sound fruit. For every tree can be told by its fruit; people do not pick figs from thorns, nor gather grapes from brambles. A good man draws what is good from the store of goodness in his heart, a bad man draws what is bad from the store of badness. For a man's words flow out of what fills his heart" (Luke 6: 43–4).

Throughout His ministry, Jesus revealed He truly was the Son of God; through His teachings, His words, coupled with Spiritual healings meant that the blind began to see, the deaf hear, and the dumb speak of Jesus as the Saviour; the Lord. When the question was put to Jesus by the rich man, "Good master, what must I do to inherit eternal life?" Jesus replied with a penetrating question, "Why do you call me good? No one is good but God alone." And although initially, it looks as if Jesus is denying that He is the Son of God, He is agreeing for if He is good, and only God is good then this goodness is from the Father and the good they see in Him is because He is true God from true God. Jesus constantly, throughout His ministry, used questions in this way to help people make connections, to knit together thought patterns, to help them to come to a more comprehensive understanding of where they were in their spiritual life.

After posing the question, Jesus then went on to explain that man needed to keep the commandments. In response, the man replied that he had kept them since his earliest days, thus establishing the fact that he was a virtuous man. "Jesus looked steadily at him, and loved him, (even though He knew what was in his heart), and he said, 'There is one thing you lack.'" Again there is evidence of Jesus knowing what is in the heart but loving the man regardless. So when Jesus told the man to sell everything he owned and give to the poor, then he would be building his treasure in heaven, the man's face fell, and he went away sad. Jesus had revealed what was in his heart, his love of his riches was greater than his love of God; basically, he wanted to have his cake and eat it, so true of our attitude to God in our world today. We want to have the gain without the pain and this stems from our own heart which is so good at deceiving us. Because we recognise and believe that Jesus is the Son of God doesn't mean that we are living a life pleasing to God.

After all, it wasn't only the virtuous that recognised Jesus as the Son of God, the Lord. At the beginning of Jesus' public ministry, after He had chosen His disciples, according to Mark, "They went as far as Capernaum, and as soon as the Sabbath came, He went to the synagogue and began to teach" (1:21). "In their synagogue was a man possessed by an unclean spirit, and it shouted, 'What do you want with us Jesus of Nazareth? I know who you are: the Hoy, one of God.' But Jesus said sharply, 'Be quiet! Come out of him!' And the unclean spirit threw the man into convolutions and with a loud cry went out of him. The people were astonished that they started asking each other what it meant. 'Here is a teaching that is new' the said 'and with authority behind it; he gives orders even to unclean spirits and they obey him.' And his reputation rapidly spread everywhere, through all the surrounding Galilean countryside" (Mark 1: 23–28).

Thus according to Mark, the first public account of Jesus encountering evil happens in the synagogue, and just as in the Garden of Eden it concerns knowledge. "I know who you are, the Holy One of God" (Mark 1:25). Jesus' response was not to enter into dialogue, but immediately to use imperative verbs, 'Be quiet, Come out'. Jesus continued throughout His ministry to cast out demons and evil spirits that would possess people. In Matthew's gospel, there are many references to demons being brought to Jesus and He cured them all, driving them out with a word, a command. "When he arrived at the other side in the region of the Gadarenes, two demon-possessed men coming from the tombs met him. They were so violent that no one could pass that way" (Matthew 8:28). "A Gentile woman who lived there came to him, pleading, 'Have mercy on me, O Lord, Son of David! For my daughter is possessed by a demon that torments her severely'" (Matthew 15:22). However, Matthew also makes references to the many who were healed from bondage. "When evening came, many who were demon-possessed were brought to him, and he drove out the spirits with a word and healed all the sick" (Matthew 8:16). Thus Jesus' unique power over evil was demonstrated by all the evil spirits obeying him.

In the time of Jesus, the activity of demons and the devil was seen as a powerful influence on people's behaviour and health, so when Jesus started casting out devils and healing the sick there was confusion as to what was happening and why. After Jesus had cured a blind and dumb demoniac, the people began to question his power, "Can this really be the son of David?" (Matthew 12:24). The Pharisees quickly responded with, "The man casts out devils only through Beelzebub, the prince of devils" (Matthew 12:24).

Whilst recognising his supernatural power his opponents wrongly attributed Jesus' exorcisms to the works of Satan and not God. Beelzebub, Lord of flies, was originally the name of a Canaanite god (2 Kings 1:2) but by the time of Jesus was changed to Beelzebub, as a name for the chief of demons, or Satan. An evil that was first introduced into the Garden of Eden through the serpent, was called the devil and in 1 Kings 21:1 was given the name Satan. Jesus uses the name Satan when He replies to the accusation that He is working for Beelzebub. "Knowing what was in their minds, (discerning the evil), he said to them, 'Every kingdom divided against itself is heading for ruin; and no town, no household divided against itself can stand. Now if Satan casts out Satan, he is divided against himself; so how can his kingdom stand? And if it is through Beelzebub that I cast out devils, through whom do your own experts cast them out?'" (12:25–27) Thus Jesus points out that what they are suggesting isn't logical for if Satan uses the power of evil to remove evil then he can only expect defeat. This argument was therefore illogical. Jesus also went on to remind them that their own 'experts' were also carrying out exorcisms, and did that mean they also were working under the influence of Satan?

However, it was the final statement of Jesus, which showed that His attack on spiritual evil was a sign of the Kingdom of God and the defeat of Satan, of evil. "But if it is through the Spirit of God that I cast devils out, then know that the Kingdom of God has overtaken you. Or then how can anyone make his way into a strong man's house and burgle his property unless he had tied up the strong man first" (Matthew 12: 28–29). In this case, the strong man is the devil, Satan. Jesus was therefore not only making a clear statement, that the Kingdom of God had arrived, God, the Father and Creator was living amongst us in the form of His Son but that through His exorcisms Jesus had already overpowered Satan. The final act of good over evil was to be played out in the final week of Jesus' life on earth, or what is now known as Holy Week.

In the events of the Holy Week, Jesus shows us is that there is a very special and unique way of overcoming evil and violence, beginning with His entry into Jerusalem. Although the people were hailing Jesus as their Messiah, their saviour, who would rescue them, the Jewish people, from the Roman occupation, Jesus challenged their perception, by riding into Jerusalem on a donkey (some versions refer to a colt or ass which would have the same association). Traditionally, entering the city on a donkey symbolizes arrival in peace, rather than as a war-waging king arriving on a horse. In Zechariah, the Messiah was foretold, "Rejoice heart and soul, daughter of Zion! Shout with gladness, daughter of Jerusalem! See now your king comes to you; he is victorious, he is triumphant, humble, and riding on a donkey, on a colt, the foal of a donkey" (Zechariah 9:9–10).

The triumphal entry into Jerusalem was a significant event, and one of the few incidents in the life of Jesus which appear in all four Gospel accounts, Matthew 21:1–17; Mark 11:1–11; Luke 19:29–40; John 12:12–19. In these accounts, Jesus was openly declaring to the people that He was their King and the Messiah they had been waiting for, but His kingdom was not of this world; His battles were not with their enemies. Instead, His kingdom was spiritual, and thus His battle was with evil; a battle in which He would triumph. He was going to be victorious and triumphant over their real enemy, sin. Thus the entry into Jerusalem was the King setting off on the last stage of the war; the battle of good versus evil. However, this was not fully understood by the followers of Jesus. Those who hailed Him as King, waving palms and singing hosannas did recognise Him as the Son of David who came in the name of the Lord, but not as the saviour who would save them from their sins. They saw Him as a messianic deliverer, someone who would lead them in a revolt against Rome.

However, it wasn't just His followers that didn't understand His messianic ministry. Previously, when Jesus had asked His disciples, "But you, who do you say I am? Simon Peter spoke up, 'You are the Christ,' he said, 'the son of the living God.' Jesus praised Peter for his response saying, 'Simon son of Jonah, you are a happy man! Because it was not flesh and blood that revealed this to you but my Father in heaven'" (Matthew 16:17). Soon after this declaration, Jesus made it clear to his disciples that he was destined to go to Jerusalem and suffer grievously at the hands of the elders and chief priests and scribes, to be put to death and to be raised on the third day. Peter responded by taking Jesus aside and protesting with him. "Heaven preserve you, Lord," he said, "This must not happen to you" (Matthew 16:22). Jesus response was quite harsh but typical of earlier examples when dealing with unclean spirits. He rebuked Peter and used an imperative verb, "Get behind me, Satan! You are an obstacle in my path because the way you think is not God's way but man's" (Matthew 16:23). Although Peter had just moments before declared Jesus as the Christ, he turned from God's perspective and viewed the situation from man's perspective, which brought about the stern rebuke: "Get behind me, Satan!" Unwittingly, Peter was not setting his mind on God's plans, His purposes but instead, Peter's mind was set on the things of man, the things of the world and all its earthly values. Peter is thinking he was protecting Jesus was inadvertently being used by Satan. Satan had purposely tempted Jesus in the wilderness at the beginning of Jesus' ministry, trying to divert Him from the victory of the cross; from fulfilling the grand design of the Father and the Son. Innocently, Peter was allowing Satan to speak through him as he had not yet grasped Jesus' true Messianic purpose.

If Jesus's disciples had problems understanding his true messianic mission, so too did those lining the route into Jerusalem. They did not recognise Jesus as their Saviour, who had come to save them from their sins, but they welcomed Him out of their desire for a messianic deliverer, someone who would lead them in a revolt against Rome. Many hoped that He would be their deliverer from the enslavement of the Romans. Thus they hailed Him as King, shouting, waving palms, and singing hosannas, hailing Him as the Son of David who came in the name of the Lord. However, the week unfolded, and Jesus allowed Himself to be captured, to be mocked, beaten, humiliated, all without a word, without a mummer; without striking a blow; but instead going quietly, obediently to death, death on the cross; the death of a common criminal; the crowds quickly turned on Him. Within just a few days, their hosannas would change to cries of "Crucify Him!" (Luke 23:20–21). Those who hailed Him, at the beginning of the week as a hero, at the end of the week would reject and abandon Him. A week that began in triumph was to end in death.

Thus, this duality that entered the world through the sin of Adam and Eve, was greatly evident throughout the week of the passion, which cumulated in the crucifixion. Peace came to the world through a violent act: The paradox of the cross; which took a life but also gave life; a physical life in exchange for spiritual life. Thus the cross that appeared to be a cruel, violent denial of God, became the supreme revelation of God. In John's gospel, the paradoxes of the Cross are everywhere apparent: glory in dishonour (John 8:49-50), power in weakness (John 15:5); triumph in defeat, and that through the suffering and death (the Passion) of Jesus Christ comes to the life and joy of the Resurrection.

Life is often mysterious, confusing tragic, and cruel. The cross confronts us with this and assures us that nothing – not even death itself – can separate us from God's love in Christ, as St. Paul says. "For I am convinced that neither death nor life, neither angels nor demons, neither the present nor the future, nor any powers, neither height nor depth, nor anything else in all creation, will be able to separate us from the love of God that is in Christ Jesus our Lord" (Romans 8: 38–39). The cross, not separating but uniting us with God our Father, through the love of Jesus His son, is the ultimate sign of victory over evil; the greatest victory ever won.

Chapter Six
Faithfulness

"I will celebrate your love forever, Yahweh, age after age my words shall proclaim your faithfulness; for I claim that love is built to last forever and your faithfulness founded firmly in the heavens" (Psalm. 89).

Although the fruits of the Spirit are all connected, the order they appear in sometimes is confusing. After goodness, comes faithfulness, which seems to be incorrectly placed. Indeed following on from goodness, self-control or the controlling of our evil desires would appear to be more of a natural flow than faithfulness. However, faithfulness involves faith and consequently is pivotal to the Christian life; that principle on which the Christian life is built upon. Faith is the root word for faithfulness, a noun and according to dictionary.com, its adjective faithful has the following definitions: '*Strict* or thorough in the performances, as in a faithful worker: *True* to one's word, promises, vows: *Steady* to one's allegiance or affection, loyal: *Reliable, trusted*, or believed: Full of faith, believing'. Thus quite simply faithfulness is a virtue, which encompasses loyalty, reliability, steadfastness, never wavering in allegiance or affection, constant, trustworthiness, fidelity, all rooted in and stemming from a belief, a faith. Thus it is aligned to goodness, overlaps with goodness, and is an extension of goodness, all actions in and stemming from our belief, our creed in a one true God, a creator, who created us in love; a love which is unconditional.

Faith, "the assurance of things hoped for, the conviction of things not seen" (Hebrews 11:1) is fundamental to all we say and do as Christians. According to Chaim Bentorah in his book, 'God's love for us: A Hebrew Teacher explores the heart of God through the marriage ceremony', "Imagination sets us apart from the animal kingdom, as we are the only creatures with an imagination." Consequently, "faith is the substance of a positive imagination, something you cannot see. Believing in a God you cannot see."

Although the precise understanding of the term 'faith' differs among the various Christian traditions, there is generally an agreement that faith in Jesus, being the resurrected son of God, lies at the core of the Christian tradition, and that such faith is required to be a Christian. Our faith, our belief is summed up in the Apostle's creed which is shared by all Christians and is the nucleus of our being; our existence; our actions. It is our doctrine, which are the beliefs held and taught by the church. Indeed, it is the doctrine of the church which dictates what we are putting out faith in, what our faith looks like, and how we apply it. "Now it is impossible to please God, without faith, since anyone who comes to him must believe that he exists, and He rewards those who try and find him" (Hebrews 11:6).

I believe in God the Father Almighty; Maker of Heaven and Earth; and in Jesus Christ, His only (begotten) Son our Lord; who was conceived by the Holy Ghost, born of the Virgin Mary; suffered under Pontius Pilate, was crucified, dead, and buried; He descended into hell; the third day He rose from the dead; He ascended into heaven, and sits at the right hand of God the Father Almighty; from there He shall come to judge the living and the dead. I believe in the Holy Spirit; the holy Catholic Church; the communion of saints; the forgiveness of sins; the resurrection of the body; and the life everlasting. Amen."

Our faith is based on what is seen and unseen. The seen is that which has been passed down to us, Jesus was born of Mary; was crucified, and rose again from the dead. Some reliable witnesses made known the facts to us. When we believe in Jesus, we believe in all He taught; that He had the power to forgive sins; life eternal for all those who believe that He was truly the son of God the Father; and that the Holy Spirit who was revealed to us through His ministry would be given to all believers; to all who asked to receive His Holy Spirit. However, it is the unseen which challenges us: God created heaven and earth; Jesus Christ is His only begotten son who was conceived by the Holy Spirit.

Thus Faith is stepping out into the unknown, accepting without understanding, trusting without seeing and believing in the unbelievable. Faith comes through humility, when we accept we don't have the answers; the knowledge or the wisdom. We can't believe under our own steam; we can't do it alone. We need the help of the Holy Spirit and just as the father, who asked Jesus to help his demonic son, when told,

103

"Everything is possible for those who have faith," responded with the words, "I do have faith. Help the little faith that I have" (Mark 9:24–25). We too need to admit to what little faith we have. First, we need to start with recognising the little faith that we have and then with the help of the Holy Spirit build on that faith. The core to developing our faith is to become conversant with the word of God, with the Bible. "Faith comes from hearing and hearing from the word of God" (Romans 10:17 ESV). The Jerusalem Bible uses the word preach, "So faith comes from what is preached, and what is preached comes from the words of Christ" (Romans 10:17). As St. Paul says in his letter to the Hebrews, "Only faith can guarantee the blessings that we hope for or prove the existence of the realities that at present remain unseen. It was by (this) faith that our ancestors were commended" (Hebrews 11:1–2).

In the Old Testament, which is based on faith, God spoke directly to His people, Adam and Eve, Moses, Noah, Abraham, Jonah, Elijah, Elisha, David, and so the list goes on. What is important is that they learnt to listen, to recognise the voice of God speaking to them, and then they did what God asked them to do. They recognised and responded to the Spirit of God in obedience. Thus obedience requires listening; it requires being attentive, that is, to know or become aware of the will of the other person to respond and consequently fulfil what is being requested. In Scripture obedience is not just a matter of mechanically fulfilling a command; it requires so much more, an active attitude that allows us to respond to God who reveals himself and His will. It was Noah, "a good man, (in harmony with God) a man of integrity, (an honest man having strong moral principles), among his contemporaries, and he walked with God" (Genesis 6:9), who responded in faith to the word of God. God shared His heart with Noah. "God said to Noah, 'The end has come for all things of the flesh; I have decided this, because the earth is full of violence of man's making and I will efface them from the earth. Make yourself an ark out of resinous wood (Genesis 6: 13–14). For my part I will bring a flood, and send the waters over the earth, to destroy all flesh on it, every living creature under heaven; everything on earth shall perish. But I will establish my covenant with you, and you must go onboard the ark, yourself, your sons, your wife, and your son's wives along with you. From all living creatures, from all flesh, you must take two of every kind aboard the ark, to save their lives and yours; they must be male and female (Genesis 6: 17–20). Noah did this; he did all that God had ordered him" (Genesis 6: 22). Thus Noah's faith in God, as stated previously, being attentive, listening and being obedient has become one of the major stories of the Old Testament, but it is Abraham, a descendent of Noah's who has gone down in history as one who had tremendous faith.

Abraham takes centre stage in the biblical book of Genesis as one of the greatest examples of listening and obeying in faith. His story begins with a Divine call for him to "go for yourself from your land, from your birthplace and the house of your father to the land that I will show you" (Genesis 12:1). Abram was a shepherd, who lived in Ur Mesopotamia, (what is now modern-day Iran). According to archaeology, Ur was a prosperous city with lovely homes, beautiful parks and public buildings and a place where people believed in and worshipped many gods. At the beginning of his life, Abraham was comfortable and secure in Ur, but he started to have conflicting views with those around him. According to the Torah, Abraham was the first person to teach the idea that there was only one God. Quite ironically, Abraham's father, Terach had initially made his living selling idols of various gods but had come to see the error of his ways and when the time came encouraged Abram to respond to God's calling. Although it is unclear how Abram comes to believe in one God, when God called him, he not only responded but throughout the rest of his life acknowledged the reality of a one true God.

"Yahweh said to Abram (who was later to be called Abraham), 'Leave your country, your family and our father's house, for the land I will show you. I will make you a great nation; I will bless you and make your name so famous that it will be used as a blessing.' So Abram went as Yahweh told him, and Lot went with him. Abram was seventy-five years old when he left Haran. He took his wife, Sarai, (later called Sarah), "his nephew Lot, all the possessions they had amassed and the people they had acquired in Haran. They set off for the land of Canaan and arrived there" (Genesis 12: 1–6).

Following God's call was anything but easy for them. When Abraham, Sarah and nephew Lot arrived in Canaan, severe hunger forced them to go down to Egypt, where Sarah was abducted by King Pharaoh. After being punished by God, Pharaoh realized that he was dealing with holy people and sent them off with great riches. Abram returned to the Negeb in the land of Canaan, and it was here that Abraham's shepherds quarrelled with Lot's shepherds, and the two relatives agreed to part ways, with Lot travelling to what was to become known as the evil city of Sodom.

After parting company with Lot, Yahweh spoke to Abram, "Look all around from where you are towards the north and the south, towards the east and the west. All the land within sight I will give you and your descendants forever" (Genesis13:14). "Later when God spoke to Abram in a vision he confirmed, 'Have no fear, Abram I am your shield your reward will be great.' Abram then voiced his concern, 'My Lord Yahweh,' Abram replied, 'What do you intend to give me? I go childless…' Then taking him outside he (God) said, 'Look up to heaven and count the stars if you can. Such will be your descendants'" (Genesis 15: 1–6). Abraham put his faith in Yahweh, he believed in his promise and so it came to be. When Abraham was ninety-nine years old, God gave him a new name: 'Abraham' – 'a father of many nations', and gave him the covenant of what has since become known as the covenant of circumcision. Abraham was told that his wife Sari, (whose name means quarrelsome), should be known in future as Sarah (princess of many) and that she would have a son.

Shortly after this revelation, Abraham and Sarah were visited by three men, one of whom told Abraham that upon his arrival next year, Sarah would have a son. While at the tent entrance, Sarah heard what was said, and she laughed out loud then denied laughing. Although the agreed reason for her laughter was that at her age, in her nineties, she was to have a child isn't clear. Her laughter could have come from a cry of joy and delight at becoming a mother at such a late age, but more importantly that God had answered her prayer. Her denial could have come from having broken protocol and eavesdropping on a male conversation. Whatever the true reason for her laughter Sarah soon became pregnant and bore a son to Abraham, at the very moment which had been predicted.

It was faith that made Abraham obey when God called him to go out to a country that God had promised to give him. He left his own country without knowing where he was going. By faith, he lived as a foreigner in the country that God had promised him. He lived in tents, as did Isaac and Jacob, who received the same promise from God. It was faith that made Abraham able to become a father, even though he was too old and Sarah herself could not have children. Not only had Abraham faith but it was this faith that caused him to trust implicitly in God to keep his promise. Though Abraham was practically dead, from this one man came as many descendants as there are stars in the sky, as many as the numberless grains of sand on the seashore. And most importantly Abraham acted through faith, when God called him and asked him to sacrifice his only, longed for, miraculous son, Isaac.

"It happened that sometime later God put Abraham to the test, 'Abraham, Abraham,' he called. 'Here I am,' he replied. 'Take your son', God said, 'Your only son Isaac, whom you love, and go to the land of Moriah. There you shall offer him as a burnt offering, on a mountain I will point out to you'" (Genesis 22: 1–3). Abraham didn't question God, even though his son whose descendants were going to make Abraham the father of many nations; his descendants as numerous as the stars in the sky; was to be sacrificed, be put to death.

In blind obedience and complete trust, "Rising early next morning Abraham saddled his ass and took with him two of his servants and his son Isaac. He chopped wood for the burnt offering and started on his journey to the place God had pointed out to him" (Genesis 22: 1–3). Torn between love for his child and obedience to God, Abraham faced agonising choices. However, he did not waver and the fact that Isaac was bound and had allowed himself perhaps, to be bound, implied he went as a willing victim. It was only when Abraham raised the knife that an angel of the Lord called to him from heaven, "Abraham, Abraham, - do not raise your hand against the boy," the angel said. "Do not harm him, for now, I know you fear God. You have not refused me your son, your only son" (Genesis 22: 11–13). In this instance, 'fear' means so much more than respecting the wishes of God. Abraham demonstrated in this action, his closeness to the heart of God. Thus, not wanting to upset or hurt the heart of God by disobedience, by sin, he was willing to sacrifice his son; his only son.

In the New Testament, however, there is more to the sacrifice of Isaac than the supreme example of complete obedience. In the letter to the Hebrews, it is said that "It was by faith that Abraham set out for a foreign country" to the promised land: "It was equally by faith that Sarah, in spite of being past the age, was made able to conceive, because she believed that he who made the promise would be faithful to it (Hebrews 11:11). It was faith that Abraham when put to the test, offered up Isaac (11:17). It was by this same faith that this same Isaac gave his blessing to Jacob and Esau for the near distant future (11:20). The letter goes on to name Moses, Gideon, Barak, Samson, Jephthah, David, Samuel, and the prophets, "heroes of faith, but they did not receive what was promised, since God had made provision for us to have something better, and they were not to reach perfection except with us" (Hebrews 11:39–40). What God had promised through His prophets, was that He would come and live among us, be one of us. Throughout the Old Testament, the holy people lived for this promise, and it is in New Testament where the prophecy, the promise, is fulfilled.

In Luke's account of the birth of Jesus, he includes Jesus being presented in the temple. When Joseph and Mary took Jesus up to Jerusalem to present him to the Lord, as laid down by the Law of Moses, they encountered Simeon, 'an upright and devout man'; he looked forward to Israel's comforting and the Holy Spirit rested on him. It had been revealed to him by the Holy Spirit that he would not see death until he had set eyes on Christ the Lord. Believing the promise and, "prompted by the Holy Spirit, he came to the temple; and when the parents brought in the child Jesus to do for him what the law required, he took him into his arms and blessed God; and he said, 'Now master you can let your servant go in peace, just as you promised; because my eyes have seen the salvation which you have prepared for all nations to see, a light to enlighten the pagans and the glory of your people Israel'" (Luke 2: 25–32).

Simeon under divine revelation recognised and embraced Jesus, while expressing his gratitude to God and a readiness to die, as the promise God had made had been fulfilled. God had sent a saviour for all people, as had been prophesied in the Old Testament. Throughout His ministry, Jesus shared His faith, His absolute trust in God the Father, with all. He frequently spoke of faith and the power of belief, often linking faith to healing. In Matthew's gospel, chapter nine, there are three stories of healing attributed to faith.

"While he was still speaking to them, up came one of the officials, who bowed low in front of him and said, 'My daughter has just died but come and lay your hands on her and her life will be saved.' Jesus rose and with his disciples, followed him"(Matthew 9:18–19).

Without question, or hesitation, Jesus immediately got up and willingly went with the man, allowing the man to lead him into what from all appearances could be termed an impossible situation, the child was already proclaimed dead. That to Jesus was not a deterrent but an opportunity to proclaim His faith, His belief that God the Father was with Him. "He who sent me is with me and has not left me to myself" (John 8:29). God, the Father, through His Spirit, was in Jesus, and thus nothing was impossible, and this becomes more evident in the next healing.

As Jesus and His disciples were following the man, "Then from behind him came a woman who had suffered for twelve years with constant bleeding. She touched the fringe of his robe, for she thought, "If I can just touch his robe, I will be healed."

Jesus turned around, and when he saw her he said, "Daughter, be encouraged! Your faith has made you well." And the woman was healed at that moment (Matthew 9:20-23). The same story is told in Luke's gospel but with more information. "Now there was a woman suffering from a haemorrhage for twelve years, whom no one had been able to cure. She came up behind him and touched the fringe of his cloak, and the haemorrhage stopped at that instant. Jesus said, 'Who touched me?' When they all denied that they had, Peter and his companions said, 'Master it is the crowds around you pushing.' They hadn't recognised the significance of what had just happened, so Jesus went on to explain, 'Someone touched me. I felt the power that had gone out from me'" (Luke 9: 43–47). Jesus was filled with power, the power of the Holy Spirit.

"Seeing herself discovered, the woman came forward trembling" (Luke 9:47). The woman was very afraid, for just like Sarah, she had broken protocol. Due to her continual bleeding, under the Mosaic Law, she would have been regarded as a woman menstruating, and consequently ceremonially unclean. To be regarded as clean, the flow of blood would have needed to have ceased for at least seven days. Thus because of the constant bleeding, this woman lived in a continual state of uncleanness which would have brought upon her social and religious isolation.

However, when challenged, and although very afraid she courageously came forward, "and falling at his feet explained in front of all the people why she had touched him and how she had been cured at that very moment. Instead of giving her a public rebuke and treating her as an outcast, Jesus does the opposite. He calls her 'My daughter', not just a family member; but a daughter who is regarded as a 'precious' family member. 'Your faith has restored you to health; go in peace'" (Luke 8:48). Jesus responded to the faith the woman had possessed. He called her into the open, restored her self-respect and established a personal relationship with her. She reached out to Jesus, and he responded. However there were incidences when the person couldn't reach out to Jesus, and He reached out to them.

After the woman with the haemorrhage was healed, Jesus continued on his journey to the Official's home. This was a man of high ranking, who in desperation, sought Jesus, not for himself but for the daughter he obviously loved. He interceded on her behalf. Coming humbly before Jesus, bowing low, the official asked Jesus to lay hands on the girl. Obviously, he had heard tales of how Jesus had healed through touch, and although he may not have witnessed the miracles, he was showing implicit faith in the power of Jesus to heal, to even bring back to life someone who was considered dead. His actions and words showed the depth of his belief, brought on no doubt through his desperate situation as he had nowhere else to turn to for help.

"When Jesus arrived at the official's home, he saw the noisy crowd and heard the funeral music. 'Get out!' He told them, 'The girl isn't dead; she's only asleep.' But the crowd laughed at him. After the crowd was put outside, however, Jesus went in and took the girl by the hand, and she stood up!" (Matthew 9:18–25). After mocking him, the crowd was dismissed by Jesus. Then in silence, He reached out and took the girl's hand. His touch transformed her life, changed it from death into life. The power of faith and intercession changed an impossible situation.

After the girl was brought back to life, Jesus went on his way where he encountered two blind men. They followed him blindly, in the dark, calling out to him to have mercy. "Take pity on us, Son of David" (Matthew 9:27). In their state of blindness, they had heard about Jesus and recognised Him as the Messiah, the descendant of David. Jesus didn't immediately heal them but when they reached the house, Jesus tested their faith, "Do you believe I can do this?" (Matthew 9: 28) So often, we can act as though we have great faith, but deep down there is the little voice saying, "It's impossible, God will do it for others, but it is a lot to ask." Jesus challenges that faith, that belief in His power. When the blind men replied, "Sir, we do," Jesus touched their eyes saying, "Your faith deserves it, so let this be done for you." Their faith was rewarded, "And their sight returned" (Matthew 9:30).

Later in Matthew's gospel when the disciples had failed to cure a man possessed with demons, Jesus rebuked them saying, "You faithless and perverse generation" (Matthew 17:17). The disciples, upset came independently to Jesus and asked why they couldn't cast out the devil. Jesus' reply was "Because you have little faith" (Matthew 17:20). He then went on to explain how a small amount of faith could change impossible situations. "I tell you solemnly if your faith were the size of a mustard seed you could say to this mountain, 'move from here to there,' and it would move; nothing would be impossible for you" (Matthew 17: 20–21).

A 'modern' day example of the faith Jesus was speaking about happened in Ohio in 1853. In desperation, the farmers in Ohio, in danger of losing their stock through an extended drought, invited the famous evangelist, and renowned father of modern revivalism, Charles Finney, 'to come and, quite simply, pray for rain'.

When the Evangelist arrived, he walked into the town carrying an umbrella. He reportedly confronted the whole community gathered in the town square, with the words, "I see I am the only one who brought an umbrella." After preaching a short sermon on faith, he then prayed, "Lord we do not presume to tell you what is best for us. You invite us to come to you as children to a father and tell you of all of our wants. We need rain. Unless you give us rain our cattle will die and our harvest will come to nought. It is an easy thing for you to do, O Lord, send us rain." God immediately answered his prayer, the prayer of a man filled with faith, interceding on behalf of those with little faith, for as he pointed out no one came with an expectation of rain, of having their prayer heard.

What is interesting to note was that Charles Finney had recognised that the people had little faith, so before he began to pray he gave a short sermon, to build up what little faith they had, presumably focusing attention onto Jesus, the miracle worker and to take their attention off Charles the evangelist. Then what is most noteworthy is the way in which he prayed.

The official when he asked Jesus to come and heal his daughter, used the words, "Come and lay your hands on her." Not only was he asking Jesus to heal his daughter but was also telling Jesus how to heal her. Jesus did what was asked but not by laying hands on the girl but by taking her by the hand. Unfortunately, we too tend to do the same, we start by telling Jesus our problem, then finish by telling Him how we want it solved, what we want Him to do. We need to pray, with faith and in humility like Charles Finney; we should not make presumptions. We need to follow the structure of Charles Finney's prayer, and pray in faith, with trust and humility, but more importantly without assumptions, assuming we know what is best in the situation. We should not tell God how to act in answering our prayers; our requests.

Easier said than done! Even the disciples of Jesus fell into that trap. "When evening came, the disciples went to him and said, "This is a lonely place, and the time has slipped by; so send the people away, and they can go to the villages to buy themselves some food" (Matthew 14: 15–16). With real empathy and concern for the people, the disciples were interceding on their behalf, but they were telling Jesus how he should act. "Jesus replied, 'There is no need for them to go: give them something to eat yourselves'" (Matthew 14:16). Of course, what happened after this dialogue has since become known as the miracle of the loaves and fishes. In this part of the story lies a huge lesson for us when we present a need to Jesus, either for ourselves or others, we just need to hand the problem to Him, no matter how big or how small, and use the words:

Lord may you be glorified in this situation. May your will be done.

It does not matter if we are praying for issues surrounding Brexit or a sore thumb, a healing for terminal cancer, or a difficult decision we have to make. The prayer is always the same. By praying as such, we are not telling God, how we want Him to act, nor are we limiting His power. Just as in the miracles of the loaves or fishes, He can answer prayers in a way we could never imagine, and all because we are asking that He may be glorified in the situation. This simple prayer can move mountains and help us regain our peace of mind while living in faith and trust. It also allows us to be persistent in prayer. After initially praying, 'may you,' then we can continue praying, with faith and confidence,

Praise and thank you that you will be glorified in this situation.

When we pray in this way, our prayers will be answered and thus not only will it increase our faith, but it will help to increase the faith of those around us.

Throughout the ages, it has been the people of faith like Charles Finney, Billy Graham, Saint Augustine, Saint Ignatius, and the list goes on, people that have helped others grow in faith, that have become noteworthy. However, there needs to be an awareness that because we are working in faith and being faithful to our beliefs doesn't mean that we are building up the kingdom of God, indeed it can mean there are times, as in the case of St. Paul that we are damaging the kingdom.

In his letter to the Galatians, Paul states, "You must have heard of my career as a practising Jew, how merciless I was persecuting the Church of God, how much damage I did to it, how I stood out among the Jews of my generation, and how enthusiastic I was for the traditions of my ancestors" (Galatians 1: 13-14). Paul cites the reason for his actions. He fully supported and carried out the persecution of Christians, until he experienced a dramatic conversion on the road to Damascus. The word, 'conversion' is disputed in this case as it implies rejecting one whole system of beliefs and embracing another, which is not what Paul did. Paul was not called to reject Judaism, but to accept Jesus as the fulfilment of all he believed. He didn't waver in allegiance or affection but was steadfast in his belief. He was faithful to the God he loved.

Sometimes, we, like Paul, can get so entrenched in our thoughts, our beliefs that we too become a hindrance in building up the kingdom of God. Our spiritual growth becomes stilted and eventually begins to wither. We become like the diseased tree, standing tall and proud, with the core being eaten away with decay and thus when the storm comes, we the rotten tree, will be the first to fall. To keep us healthy we need to be faithful, loyal, and steadfast, to be continually growing in faith, and to do this we need to allow ourselves to be led and guided, daily, by the Holy Spirit, listening to the promptings of His words, and allowing the Holy Spirit to reveal the Sacred Scriptures to us.

Chapter Seven
Gentleness

"Do not dress up for show: doing up your hair, wearing gold bracelets and fine clothes; all this should be inside, in a person's heart, imperishable: the ornament of a sweet and gentle disposition – this is what is precious in the sight of God." (1 Peter 3: 3–5)

The penultimate fruit of the Spirit, according to Paul, is gentleness. Unsurprisingly, it is a word that can't be said harshly but is always spoken quietly, almost reverently. Perhaps the reason for this is because its synonyms are: 'kindness, tenderness, mercy, forgiveness, forbearance; sympathy, considerateness, understanding, compassion, kind-heartedness, tender-heartedness, good nature, love; quietness, mildness, modesty, humility, stillness, tranquillity, reverence, meekness, docility', to name but a few! Thus, gentleness links the other fruits of peace, patience, kindness, goodness, and self-control with one central element, the love of others and not of oneself. It is similar to kindness, but with an added addition, that of cultivating a softness of heart towards other people and putting that into action by the way we speak and behave towards them. Somehow, we have come to view gentleness and meekness, as a weakness when in fact it is the opposite, it is a strength.

A lovely story that illustrated this point was found in the 'Wide Range Readers Book 3', a collection of stories used in teaching children how to read. It told the story of the wind and the sun trying to decide who was the stronger and who was the weaker.

One day, the wind challenged the sun to a contest as he claimed he was quite simply the stronger of the two. The wind looked down and seeing a man walking along turned to the sun and stated that the stronger one would be able to remove the coat from the man. The sun agreed to the contest and the competition went ahead with the wind going first. Mustering all the strength and force that was possible, the wind blew and blew, harder and harder. However, the harder he blew the more the man pulled the coat around him. Eventually, the wind had to admit defeat and so the sun took her place. She shone gently down on the man. As her rays penetrated the earth, the man became hot and without any force used, he removed his coat. Thus the moral of the story was that brute force was unnecessary and even detrimental to achieving the goal, whereas all that was needed was a gentle persuasion.

Concealed in the story was the important use of pronouns. Unlike the French language, our nouns are not classified as masculine or feminine. In the English language, we are given the freedom to attribute the male and female traits and yet unknowingly we do tend to use much the same criteria and attribute certain aspects to males and females. Consequently, female traits are normally associated in Western society as those which encompass gentleness, empathy, sensitivity, caring, compassion, tolerance, nurturance, whereas the male traits include protection, providing, strength, both physical and that of strong character, courage, independence, even violence, and assertiveness. And thus it is unsurprising that the wind in the story is referred to as, 'he', whereas the sun is referred to as 'she'. However, this concealed, unspecified, classification doesn't only happen in stories but is also evident in the Bible and in turn limits our understanding of God as a gentle loving father.

Throughout the Old Testament, the strong, protective nature of God is emphasised; the masculine nature of God. In Isaiah we learn, "(For) Yahweh consoles his people and takes pity on those afflicted" (Isaiah 49: 13). According to Chaim Bentorah in his book, 'Hebrew Study Beyond the Lexicon', sometimes the choice of the words, when translating the Bible from Hebrew, incorporated those which emphasised the more masculine nature of God; that of being strong, protective, and powerful rather than incorporating a more feminine side; that of being gentle, caring, soft or tender-hearted. In using certain words, the translators were deliberately portraying a strong, powerful but unfortunately relatively unemotional God.

This discrepancy is apparent in Isaiah where later in the chapter is given a greater, beautiful, more powerful image; the love of God equated to that of a mother. "Does a mother forget her baby at the breast, or fail to cherish the son of her womb? Yet even if these forget, I will never forget you" (Isaiah 49: 15-16). It is in verses like these we glimpse the gentleness, the tenderness of God our Father. God treats us with such gentleness and just like the sun, He uses His love, not force, to transform us, to guide us. No one knew this more than David when he wrote Psalm 23, The Lord is my Shepherd. David, a shepherd, used this analogy as he was able to recognise similar traits, in the way a shepherd would care for his sheep to that of how we are cared for by a loving, gentle Father.

The Psalm even begins with the words, "Yahweh is my shepherd I lack nothing." (Jerusalem Bible.) David, initially, was a shepherd boy who took care of his father's flock, and consequently knew exactly what he meant when he used this metaphor of God in the role of a shepherd. He was referring to the special relationship between the sheep and the shepherd, a very close and intimate one. It is also one of dependency, where the sheep relies totally on the shepherd for provision, guidance, and protection. Thus by referring to God as a shepherd, David was recognising this dependency; in his feebleness, he needed God's power, in his weakness he needed God's strength, in his inability he needed God to provide for him.

Although sheep are widely considered as herbivores, feeding on grass and clover and pasture plants, this is not always the case. According to a report in the Independent online, Monday 18 February 2002, Zoologists have observed sheep eat meat in the wild to boost diet. In places where their normal diet is low in essential minerals, they have been seen eating grouse and seabird chicks. Hence, when we pray this Psalm like David, this lovely metaphor takes on a deeper meaning for us, as it does not matter where we are, in what conditions, God will provide us with what we need, so not only our spiritual life but also our physical life may be nourished and grow. God will provide the essentials if we can learn to trust Him like a sheep has total trust in the shepherd.

And just as a shepherd, in Middle Eastern countries, leads his flock, walks in front, with them trustingly following behind so will God lead us, not force us, but gently lead the way, into tranquillity and away from danger, into "meadows of green grass where he lets me lie" (Psalm 23). David uses the word green, the colour which has an association with life, renewal, nature, and energy. It is a word that is also associated with growth, harmony, freshness, safety, fertility, and the environment, and it is into this positive place, flowing with energy David is allowed to rest, to stop and recuperate, recharge his batteries. Then, "To the waters of repose, He leads me; there he revives my soul." The word 'water' as stated earlier, is used in a variety of metaphorical ways in Scripture, with the symbolism of water often being associated with purity and fertility; water is viewed as the source of life itself. Thus in this verse, there is more than just life-giving refreshment, water is seen as doing so much more; it renews, restores, refreshes the soul, or the spirit; linking it therefore to a rebirth. A relationship to God leads to a spiritual rejuvenation, a renewal of the very essence of our being for like the sheep we can recognise our vulnerability and also recognise our need for protection in our daily lives.

For a sheep, protection is extremely important. Unlike all other animals that have a special way to defend themselves, sheep don't possess this mechanism; they don't have any fighting skills, which makes them the only animals on earth that are defenceless. Consequently, they are vulnerable, being at the end of the food chain. David recognises this vulnerability, this dependency on the shepherd, when he claims, "Though I pass through a gloomy valley, I fear no harm; beside me, your rod and staff are there to hearten (comfort) me" (Psalm 23:4). David, who had previously described how he had used the rod as a means of protecting the sheep, when asking Saul's permission to fight the Philistines said, "Your servant used to look after the sheep for his father and whenever a lion or a bear came out and took a sheep from the flock, I used to follow him up and strike him down, and rescue it from his mouth; if he turned on me I seized him by the hair at his jaw and struck him down and killed him" (1 Samuel: 34-–). Thus, there is the ambiguity of the gentleness of the shepherd with the violent, aggressive act needed to ward off danger. The rod was used as a form of protection from all danger, but only as a means of a last resort. David recognised that God possesses this absolute power to protect us from all danger, ward off all evil, especially when we are at our most vulnerable, our weakest. The darker the shadow, the closer the Lord.

As well as the rod, the second essential piece of shepherding equipment is a staff; a long stick with a crook on the end. Waiving the staff with an outstretched arm, helped to block the sheep, from going down the wrong route. It gave the shepherd a longer arm and reach and thus was more effective in helping to steer them in the right direction. In addition to this, the crook allowed the shepherd to gently catch the weak, limping, and pregnant sheep, rather than chasing after them, which would cause sheep a lot more stress. Another very gentle use of the crook was to return a lamb to its mother. Consequently, both the rod and the staff are essential tools for the shepherd, to protect, guide, lead, and rescue the sheep, getting them out of all difficulties, both young and old. So in Psalm 23, when David, who was a great and mighty king with an army, used the metaphor of God as a shepherd, he was able to recognise the helpless state of his humanity; his nothingness; his vulnerability; his total dependency on a God who, like a shepherd combines both the feminine traits of gentleness and caring, with the masculine traits of a protector, a provider, a leader, and a guardian.

David often likened the relationship between God and us as a shepherd to his sheep, "Shepherd of Israel listen, you who lead Joseph like a flock" (Psalm 80:1). "For this is our God, and we are the people he pastures, the flock that he guides" (Psalm 95:7), attributed to David in Hebrews (4:7). However, he was not the only one to make this connection, as the theme of shepherd and sheep appears constantly throughout the Old Testament. "With shepherd's crook lead your people to pasture, the flock that is your heritage" (Micah 7:14).

And when God spoke through His prophets, he also used the metaphor of shepherd and sheep: "I am going to look after the flock myself and keep it all in view" (Ezekiel 34:11). In the following verses, this is explained as; "Keep my sheep in view" (34:12); "rescue them, gather them, bring them back; pasture them; I will feed them; I will show them where to rest; look for the lost one; bring back the stray; bandage the wounded, and make the weak strong. I shall be a true shepherd to them" (Ezekiel 34: 12–17). What a beautiful picture is being painted in this prophecy! The picture of the gentleness of the shepherd to the sheep and in return the trust of the sheep towards the shepherd. Isaiah, in his messianic prophecies also used this analogy, "He is like a shepherd feeding his flock, gathering lambs in his arms, holding them against his breast and leading to their rest the mother ewes" (Isaiah 40:11).

God kept his promise and just as Isaiah had prophesied, came to live among us as a Good Shepherd. Although Jesus referred to himself only once, in John's Gospel, as the Good Shepherd, there is evidence throughout His ministry of Jesus ministering to the people as a shepherd would minister to his flock. Indeed Jesus even told a parable about a wandering sheep, which appears in the Gospel of Matthew (18:12–14) and a lost sheep which is found in Luke's (15:3–7). In both gospels, a shepherd leaves his flock of ninety-nine sheep to find the one which is lost, or who has just wandered off.

The parable begins with a straying sheep. A sheep separated from its shepherd is defenceless and in grave danger. By using this analogy, Jesus is referring to sin, which draws us into the darkness and cuts us off, alienates us from God the Father, leaving us groping around aimlessly in darkness, our spiritual soul in mortal danger. "So justice is far from us, and righteousness does not reach us. We look for light, but all is darkness; for brightness, but we walk in deep shadows" (Isaiah 59:9). The fact that the shepherd goes looking for the sheep is not only very beautiful for us but reassuring that God does not give up on us or abandon us when we have strayed or wandered away and turned our backs on Him.

In the parables, Jesus was not only reassuring us about the Father's concern when we are lead into sin but is emphasising the fact, that although a shepherd may not be that concerned for a missing sheep, this certainly was not the case with His Father, who deeply loves and cares personally for us as individuals. We are so valuable to him he will seek far and wide to bring us back home, to be with Him. He doesn't punish us or treat us harshly; doesn't take pleasure in our sins or admonish us, but joyfully welcomes us back. In Luke's gospel, there is an added addition to the parable, "And when he found it, would he not joyfully take it on his shoulders and then when he got home, call together his friends and neighbours. 'Rejoice with me,' he would say, 'I have found my sheep that was lost' (Luke 15:5–7). He takes the sheep on his shoulder, he shoulders the burden, doesn't force the sheep to go back to the flock, but carries the weak and vulnerable, not with anger or rapprochement, but with joy and love.

What is surprising about this parable is that it was told by Jesus to the Pharisees and religious leaders after they had accused him of welcoming and eating with 'sinners'. The Jewish culture was a shame/honour-driven society. Virtually, every act was seen in the light of either bringing shame or honour. Consequently, the primary motivation for what and how things were done was based on seeking honour for oneself and avoiding shame. This was the central and all-consuming preoccupation of all Jewish interaction. Thus the Pharisees when criticising Jesus, were being hypocritical; refusing to acknowledge their sins but judging others, and condemning Jesus as they felt He was acting in a shameful and not honourable way; by his association with the tax collectors and sinners. Jesus uses this parable therefore as a model of pastoral concern, demonstrating the Father's mercy and compassion towards us. He also uses it to teach us that this is the way in which we need to treat others, in a loving, non-judgemental way.

Although there may be a temptation to look down on less confident, or successful fellow disciples and to ignore their pastoral needs, this should not be the case because it shows an attitude out of tune with God's concern, His mercy, the way He treats us. Indeed the early Christians regarded this parable as a call for us to be concerned for all the lost sheep, especially those who have wandered away from the flock and to put that concern into action (James 5:19). We need to take the burden of separation upon our shoulders, and carry it back to Jesus, not just in thought but in prayer, and work tirelessly for unity, in prayer, word and deed. After all, God did warn us about false shepherds, or those through wanton neglect allowed wolves to attack the sheep.

Interestingly, Jesus starts this parable with the words, "I am the Good Shepherd," and thus makes this distinction, highlighting that not all shepherds are good, which had been foretold by the prophets. Throughout the Bible, there are examples of neglectful shepherds, ones who brought dishonour to their name. In Jeremiah, the prophet castigates the bad shepherds of Israel, for not attending to their flocks with true pastoral care, "They have scattered the sheep, neglected the flock, and led them astray among the nations" (Jeremiah 23:5). Where pastoral care is described as not just physical but as emotional and spiritual support that can be found in all cultures and traditions, it often has different meanings in the Bible. Today, in our modern context it is described as supporting people not only in their pain, loss, and anxiety, but also in their triumphs, joys, and victories.

In Ezekiel, we learn more about the bad shepherds and how they do not fulfil their pastoral role or duty of care, as it is often called. The image of the people as a flock of sheep occurs several times throughout the Bible and in this instance, Ezekiel is speaking about the people and the rulers of Israel. "Trouble for the shepherds of Israel who feed themselves! Shepherds ought to feed their flock, yet you have fed on milk, you have dressed yourself in wool, you have sacrificed the fattest sheep, but failed to feed the flock" (Ezekiel 34: 2–3). These leaders had become self-indulgent, putting their own needs, wants and desires first whilst ignoring the needs of others. "You have failed to make the weak strong, or to care for the sick or lost ones, or bandaged the wounded ones" (34:4). Thus, their actions had caused them to neglect the needy, and this lack of care caused many to be lost, to wander away wounded into further danger. As Ezekiel continues, "You have failed to bring back strays or look for the lost. On the contrary, you have ruled them cruelly and violently" (34:4). Thus the gentleness of a good shepherd is contrasted with the violence and destruction of the bad shepherd. Those people, especially in a position of power, who had acquired their wealth and power by oppressing and bullying the poor, weak, defenceless, and vulnerable were being compared to bad shepherds. However, the prophets claimed that the situation would not be allowed to continue. The warning turns into a promise for the future, "I mean to raise up one shepherd, my servant, David, and to put him in charge of them and he will pasture them; he will pasture them and be their shepherd. I, Yahweh, will be their God, and my servant David shall be their ruler" (Ezekiel 34: 23-24).

As in other prophecies, the name David is symbolic. The reference to David does not refer to the ancient king but to someone, the Lord delights in and is triumphant over the foes of Israel, over the evil that is pervading God's people. Jesus came to teach us, all of us how we too can become true shepherds within our community. Pope Francis, on 27th September 2017, the Feast of St. Vincent de Paul, stated quite forcibly that charity is central to the Church's mission, and we are called to share it with the world, especially those in need: "All of us, in truth, are called to water ourselves upon the rock that is the Lord and to quench the world's thirst with the charity that springs from Him. Charity is at the heart of the

Church, it is the reason for its action, the soul of its mission."
In the parable of The Good Samaritan, Jesus explains to us
how we can minister to the needs of others, show our duty of
care.

In response to a question asked by a lawyer, "And who is
my neighbour? (Luke10: 25) Jesus told the story of a traveller,
who while on his way from Jerusalem to Jericho was attacked.
He was stripped of clothing, beaten, and left half dead
alongside the road. First, a priest and then a Levite came by,
but both avoided the man, possibly they feared defilement
through touching a dead body. The next person who came
along was a Samaritan, not only was he a non-Jewish man but
Samaritans and Jews despised each other. And in the parable
it was this Samaritan man who, 'moved by compassion',
'bandaged his wound'. (Just as Ezekiel had prophesied, "I will
bandage the wounded.") and then poured oil, (healing) and
wine on them." Oil and wine were symbolic of the Holy
Spirit, of the fullness of joy and divine grace. "He then lifted
him, just as a shepherd would lift a wounded sheep, 'carried
him', took him in his arms and held him (close to his heart).
The next day he paid the innkeeper, two denarii. 'Look after
him,' he said, 'And on my way back I will make good any
extra expense you have'" (Luke 10: 33-36). Thus, Jesus was
telling us to go that extra mile; to confront the needy, not to
avoid them and do it out of love.

There are also parallels in this story with the life of Jesus.
He came and made His home with us and out of love took on
out debt, paid with his life for our sins. "I am the good
shepherd; the good shepherd is the one who lays down his life
for his sheep" (10:11,14-17). As Isaiah in a messianic
prophesy said, "We had all gone astray like sheep, each taking

his way, and Yahweh burdened him with the sins of all of us. Harshly dealt with, he bore it humbly, he never opened his mouth, like a lamb that is led to the slaughterhouse, like a sheep that is dumb before its shearers never opening its mouth" (Isaiah 53:6–8).

Sheep are the only animals that do not make noise when they die, they do not complain when they need to be sacrificed, they do not get angry and they do not try to escape, all of which summons up Jesus' betrayal, arrest, and consequent death.

While on the cross and dying, Jesus was still full of concern for others. "Near the cross of Jesus stood his mother and his mother's sister, Mary, the wife of Clopas, and Mary of Magdala. Seeing his mother and the disciple he loved standing near her, Jesus said to his mother, 'Woman, this is your son.' Then to the disciple, he said, 'This is your mother.' And from that moment the disciple made a place for her in his home" (John 19: 25–27). Jesus, in the hour of his greatest trial and tender consideration, committed Mary his mother, to John the beloved disciple. Mary, the mother, who had given birth to Him, nurtured Him, and whose gentle love, humility and obedience Jesus displayed in His final hours on earth.

"It was now about the sixth hour and, when the sun eclipsed, a darkness came over the whole land until the ninth hour. The veil of the temple was torn right down the middle; and when Jesus had cried out in a loud voice, he said, 'Father, into your hands I commit my spirit.' With these words, he breathed his last" (Luke 23:44-46). He said loudly so all could hear the words spoken with joy; words spoken with love and forgiveness. He was going home, back into the arms of His

Father, having accomplished His mission. "After taken the vinegar he said, 'It is accomplished'" (John 19:30).

In humility and meekness, Jesus came to, 'look for the lost sheep', those who had wandered and strayed. He wanted, echoing the words of the Psalmist, 'To rescue them' from all the dangers that ensnared them and the evil that surrounded them: 'To gather them', by calling to them. "The sheep that belong to me listen to my voice; I know them, and they follow me" (John 10:27). He came to 'Bring them back, into the flock'; not only that but to gently pick up the weak, lame, and wounded ones and carry those sheep who were weary, tired, or weak.

Continuing with His pastoral care, Jesus wanted to, "Pasture them; 'I will feed them, with my word (Matthew 4:4). I will show them where to rest;' and then lead them to tranquil, peaceful places" (John 14:27). Look for the lost one; leave the ninety-nine to go off and find the one who had inadvertently wandered away (and is unaware of their lost situation) (Matthew 18: 12–13): Bring back the stray; lead the way back into the flock, guiding them back onto the right path (Mark 10:32). I will bandage the wounded (Luke 10:34), and thus start the healing process, and make the weak strong (Isaiah 40:29); My grace is enough for you; my power is at its best in weakness" (2 Corinthians 12:12).

The mission that ended on the cross began the ministry of Jesus that prevails today. In gentleness, His Spirit ministers to us, gaining our trust. Indeed, sometimes, this fruit of the Spirit is known as trustfulness and that is the relationship between the sheep and the shepherd and needs to be the relationship we develop with our Lord, one of meekness, dependability on Him for all our needs, with a faith that is unshakeable, all wrapped up in love. We need to allow Him to take us in His arms, hold us close to His heart and minister to all our needs.

Self-Control.

"For the Spirit God gave us does not make us timid, but gives us power, love and self-discipline" (2 Timothy 1:7)

The final fruit of the Spirit is self-control, which is quite simply, the ability to control one's emotions, behaviour, and desires in the face of adversity, and although it is last it certainly is not the least, not by a long shot. In fact, it is huge!

In psychology, it is regarded as the capability to not only achieve goals but to be able to avoid impulses and emotions that could be negative. No matter how simple the definition, there is no getting away from the fact that self-control is very complex and absolutely essential if we are to produce fruit in our lives. It allows us to grow in righteousness and selflessness but more importantly, it gives us the ability to bring sin under control. It is beautifully summed up in Proverb 25, "Like a city whose walls are broken through is a person who lacks self-control" (Proverbs 25:28). And in Proverb 16, we learn, "Better a patient person than a warrior, one with self-control than one who takes a city" (Proverbs 16:32).

Through self-indulgence and lack of self-control, we can become slaves to our passions, giving in to temptations, sinning, or turning our backs on God, while all the time believing that we are in control of our emotional situations, justifying the reasons for our errant behaviour. We fall into the trap Jeremiah warned against, "The heart is more devious than any other thing, perverse too: who can know its secrets?" (Jeremiah 17:9). And in Romans, Paul states, "Do not let your love be a pretence, sincerely prefer good to evil" (Romans 12:9). Perhaps one of the most obvious examples of this deception was of David – yes David, King and Shepherd – who in the previous chapter, demonstrated by his Psalms that he was so close to God's heart; who loved God with such a passion, but even he allowed his complacency to blind him, and consequently to stumble into sin; who, due to his lack of self-control became like a city with no defences when the attack came.

The story of David and Bathsheba, in the Old Testament, reminds us of how great men who are called by God, are still humans and struggle with sin, become weak and give in to temptation. David's first interactions with Bathsheba are described in 2 Samuel 11, "David had sent his army off where they had massacred the Ammonites and laid siege to Rabbah, while he chose to stay at home in Jerusalem. One night, King David, while walking upon his rooftop spotted a beautiful woman bathing nearby (2 Samuel 11:2). David asked his servants about her and was told, 'Why that is Bathsheba, Eliam's daughter, the wife of Uriah the Hittite'" (2 Samuel 23:39).

The 'why' at the beginning of the answer implies surprise, possibly that David didn't know who this woman was, which in turn raises a few questions: Was David already aware of her existence and lusting over her? Was that the reason this mighty king, victorious in battle, had not gone off to war with his men? Was David's heart already deceiving him? Here was this beautiful, lonely woman, who he just needed to be comforted. One whose husband had cared so little for her, he had gone off and abandoned her. However, this is just presumption, but what we can be sure about, based on David's actions, is that when David 'sent messengers and had her brought' (2 Samuel 11:4) his intentions towards her were anything but honourable.

Just like David, we too can fall into this trap; of fooling ourselves into believing our motives are honourable and pure. Indeed, we have a great ability and are clever at deceiving ourselves regarding our true motives; we cover up the truth. We give in to our emotions, our passions, at a great cost, not only to our lives but to those around us, and so it was for David in his behaviour towards Bathsheba. Although Bathsheba is often regarded as the temptress, there is no evidence of this in the bible. Indeed there is more evidence to prove the contrary. As was the custom in biblical times, Bathsheba was identified by her relation to men, both her father and her husband (2 Samuel 23:39). Thus, this double identification indicates that she was a respectable person, as women with a dubious reputation were sometimes not identified by, and associated with, a named male relative. Thus not only was she married but she would have been well respected in her community.

This little fact that she was a respectable woman, did not deter David and despite knowing her marital status, he gave in to his desire and summoned Bathsheba to the palace, where they slept together. "She came to him, and he slept with her; now she had just purified herself." She then went back home again (2 Samuel 11:5). After David had sex, intercourse without love, with Bathsheba, an act that was tantamount to rape, he sent her home. Not only would it appear that he had no intention of developing a loving relationship with her, but he had abused his power, to satisfy the sins of the flesh. After all, he was her king; she his subject; her husband's boss; she could not refuse him, and he, presumably, took advantage of this, satisfied his own need, and then sent her away, defiled. David would have been very aware of the twentieth letter of the Hebrew alphabet, the Resh, which represents the head, or the leader, and the primary meaning is that a leader does not abuse his power but depends on God, not on his abilities. The letter also teaches that, if a leader does make a bad decision, he must repent, turn away from it, and never look back, as looking back can be a temptation to return to the scene of the crime and commit the offence again.

The shadow of the Resh, the negative aspect, is a warning to those who take a leadership role that power can corrupt. Leadership can easily veer towards egotism, arrogance, and corruption whether it be in our parishes, communities, or even our place of work. The 'Resh' therefore reminds us always to; be vigilant and on guard against these sometimes subtle tendencies towards abuse of that power; to repent of these tendencies immediately, and to turn away from them; to move into the direction of holiness; in reality move out of the darkness into the light.

Although David had turned his back on the 'Resh', abused his power and refused to acknowledge or repent of his downfall, he did what so many of us do, he carried on regardless as though nothing had happened and expected Bathsheba to do the same. Quite simply, after he had fed his lust, Bathsheba was expected to resume her life, as Uriah's wife, and to continue as normal. In his senseless lust, however, David seemingly did not anticipate that Bathsheba might become pregnant, even though she had just gone through seven days of purification, thus she was at her most fertile. He had abused his position of power and in denial of his misdeeds, he tried to save face, so instead of admitting the truth, he attempted to control and manipulate the situation, with disastrous consequences. David had only to look back in history to realise that trying to manipulate situations for favourable outcomes can be disastrous, just as the Israelite army learnt.

In the first book of Samuel, Chapter 4, we find the struggle of the Israelites to understand God's way as demonstrated during the battle between the Israelites and the Philistines. After a day in the battle where the Israelites were defeated and four thousand men lost their lives, the elders of Israel decided to take matters into their own hands. "Why has Israel's Yahweh allowed us to be defeated today by the Philistines? Let us fetch the ark of our God from Shiloh so that it may come amongst us and rescue us from the power of our enemies" (1 Samuel 4:3). And that is exactly what they did, they used the Ark of the Covenant, which symbolised God's presence and power to intimidate the non-believers as the Philistines believed the Ark of the Covenant was a sort of idol, a magic object which would give Israel great power in the battlefield. "When the ark of Yahweh arrived in the camp, all Israel gave a great shout so that the earth resounded. When the Philistines heard the shouting, they said, 'What can this great shouting in the Hebrew camp mean?' And they realised that the Ark of Yahweh had come into the camp. 'Alas!' They cried. 'This had never happened before. Who will save us from the power of the mighty God?'" (1Samuel: 4:5–8).

As Israel learnt that day, God was not on their side. They had invoked him, told Him how he should act and then in their desperation had tried to force God into acting in a way that was beneficial for them. However, the Philistines fought bravely and won an even bigger victory. "The slaughter was great indeed, and there fell of the Israelites thirty-thousand-foot soldiers. The ark of God was captured too, and the two sons of Eli died, Hophni and Phinehas" (1 Samuel 4:10–11).

Thankfully, we today, aren't like the Israelites, and use prayers, attendance at religious services, or almsgiving as a way and means of trying to manipulate God into doing our will and not His. Or are we? If we are truly honest with ourselves and don't let our hearts deceive us we will have to admit that we have more in common with the Israelites and David than we would like to have ourselves believe. David allowed his heart to deceive him into believing he could manipulate and control the situation. When he learnt that his sin of adultery was about to be exposed and that he a man of great faith had fallen, had betrayed the God he loved, he decided to act in a way that would be beneficial to him, but which ultimately cost lives, just as it had done the Israelites.

When David learnt that Bathsheba had become pregnant, she, "Sent word to David, 'I am with child'" (2 Samuel 11:5). He summoned Uriah from the army, in the pretence of wanting a report on the battle. His main intention, which was revealed later, was a lot more devious. He had Uriah summoned in the hope that he would have sex with Bathsheba and consequently when Uriah would find out that Bathsheba was pregnant he would have been fooled into believing the child was his. On the pretence of being a kind, considerate boss, even posing as a friend, after David had questioned Uriah about the battle, he said to him. "Go down to your house and enjoy yourself" (2 Samuel 11:8). David wanted to 'save face'; his egotism would not allow him to lose favour in mans' eyes or fall spectacularly from grace.

When Uriah came before his king, that was the golden opportunity for David to make amends, to man up to the situation, humbly admit his sin, and ask Uriah's forgiveness. Easier said than done, indeed it is one of the hardest things to do; to admit we have fallen off our pedestal, let ourselves down, and given in to Satan's temptations. Certainly, it is easier for us to admit our sin to God, in the privacy of our room and without anyone needing to know about our lapse, than to openly approach the person we have wronged, look them in the face, eye to eye, and tell them of not only how we have wronged them, but more importantly how sorry we are; and humbly ask them to forgive us. Our big stumbling block is our pride, and this is a time when in reflection we can realise, what exactly is important to us, winning glory from God or our fellow man? This is the test of our egotism, where in fact, our loyalty lies and what is really in our hearts. And no matter how difficult it is for us this is the only way forward and is vital to us if we are to grow in our Christian life. How many relationships are broken today because people will not admit to their failings, own up to the truth, and use that phrase so important, 'I am sorry'?

Where the Old Testament focuses mainly on God's forgiveness of individuals or groups, the New Testament addresses how we can and should forgive each other. Jesus often spoke about forgiveness during His ministry, but while using the word 'forgiveness', He never gave a definite meaning, and thus ambiguity has grown up around the subject, so often when people are talking about forgiveness. Some many different interruptions or myths surrounding this act. Indeed when we are told that 'you must forgive the brother who wronged you', that is true, but it is only part of the verse because nowhere in the Gospels does Jesus teach that forgiveness should be offered unconditionally. In Luke's gospel, Jesus says, "If your brother does something wrong, reprove him and, if he is sorry, forgive him. And if he wrongs you seven times a day and seven times comes back to you and says, 'I am sorry,' you must forgive him" (Luke 17:4). Forgiveness is implicitly linked to remorse, regret, and repentance, first to God and then to the person we have wronged.

We cannot expect someone to forgive us if we don't show regret and remorse for our actions but more importantly before we get to that step we need to own up, to admit to ourselves, and then to the person, what we have done wrong. We can only worship in Spirit and truth. We need to be reflective so we can be truthful to ourselves and then not only say 'sorry' from our hearts but go that one step further and show empathy to the person we have wronged, acknowledging how our transgression could have hurt them and repeating the words after each admission, 'I am sorry'. If David had asked for forgiveness in this way with true regret and remorse for what he had done it would have given Uriah the help and strength he needed to start to forgive David from 'his heart', and it would have allowed him to begin to let go and not hold onto a grudge or try to get revenge, to right the wrong. It is how we respond to the hurt caused by others that dictates our belief and faith. As the Talmudic teaches, "Those who ignore the impulse to get even, all their sins are ignored in the heavenly record."

David never attempted to go down this route of repentance instead he encouraged Uriah to go back to his home and sleep with his wife. However, Uriah refused to go home. Being a virtuous man, according to the book of Samuel, and one of integrity, Uriah followed the code laid down, where soldiers in time of battle were forbidden to have intercourse. Instead of going home, he spent the night at the palace. "Uriah however slept by the palace door with his master's bodyguard and did not go down to his house" (2 Samuel 11:9). He had thwarted David's plans but when questioned why he didn't go home, Uriah replied, "Are not the ark and the men of Israel and Judah lodged in tents; and my master Joab and the bodyguard of my Lord, are they not in the open fields? Am I to go to my house, then and eat and drink with my wife? As Yahweh lives, and as you live, I will do no such thing!" Such honourable words were spoken from a man of integrity, and did they make David guilty; guilty enough to own up and confess? Of course not! Instead of admitting his transgression, David became more determined to cover his sin. So he hatched up another plan, and this time it was to get Uriah drunk. When Uriah was inebriated David encouraged him to go home and sleep with his wife.

"The next day David invited him to eat and drink in his presence and made him drunk" (2 Samuel 11:13). However, this plan also failed, for "In the evening Uriah went out and lay on his couch with his master's bodyguard, but he did not go down to his house"(11: 13).

It soon became apparent that David's act of adultery could not be covered up and so David continued down the road of destruction, fooling himself and those around him. This time he enacted a second, more sinister plan: he commanded his military leader, Joab, to place Uriah on the front lines of battle and then to purposefully fall back from him, leaving Uriah exposed to enemy attack. In this way, only

Uriah would be killed and no other men fighting for David. "Station Uriah in the thick of the fight and then fall back behind him so that he may be struck down and die" (2 Samuel 11:15). Joab followed the directive but amended it so other men did die with Uriah. Joab must have been aware of what David was doing, too many questions would have been asked if only Uriah had died and so to ensure that David avoided a public scandal, Joab became a co-conspirer and sacrificed the life of the men who were entrusted to him. Joab had followed the instructions of his corrupt leader and sinned against God and man to help conceal David's adultery.

In Israel at that time, adultery was taken seriously and punishable by death. However, as David was the chief judge, he could not condemn himself to death, so to all concerned, the death of Uriah solved a problem. Not only did David abuse his position but in effect, he used it to gain popularity, and to present himself as a considerate king. After her time of mourning, David married the grieving, pregnant widow, thus gaining respect, instead of condemnation in peoples' eyes, and she gave birth to a son. "But what David had done displeased Yahweh" (2 Samuel 11:27) and so he was brought to a place of repentance. "I am the one who reproves and disciplines all those he loves; so repent in real earnest" (Revelations 3:19).

God sent the prophet Nathan to David. Instead of openly condemning him, Nathan spoke to him in a parable about two men, who lived in the same town, one was rich, as he had flocks and herds in abundance; whereas the other was poor, as he had nothing but a ewe lamb, which was greatly valued. This lamb grew up as part of the family, eating the poor man's bread and drinking from his cup, even sleeping on his breast.

When a traveller came, the rich man refused to take one of his flocks but took the poor man's lamb and prepared it for his guest. When David heard the story he became angry and declared the man deserved to die. "He must make fourfold restitution for the lamb, for doing such a thing and showing no compassion" (2 Samuel 12:6).

David knew that the proper penalty for a sheep was fourfold payment (Exodus 22:1) but he was greatly indignant at the evil way the rich man had behaved and so David was misled into believing that Nathan was describing a genuine incident. By his words, he had pronounced a sentence before realizing what Nathan meant, that he was describing David's behaviour with Uriah's wife, Bathsheba. Thus David had not only condemned himself but had been made aware of the realities of the situation. The position of power, as in that of a king, enabled them, the powerful, to become greedy, and to grab anything they wanted, and in return the ordinary citizen was helpless. Not only could they covet their neighbour's wife, their neighbour's goods, but they could take them, all of which are breaking the laws of God, breaking God's heart who had empowered them in the first place. "In so far as you did this to the least of my brothers of mine, you did it to me" (Matthew 25:40). Although when Jesus spoke these words he was referring to those who showed kindness to others, however, as in the two sides of the coin, if our kindness makes God happy, then our unkindness to others must make him sad, and in return, separates us from his love.

Thus when we too set out on that path of self-destruction, giving in to our passions, our jealousies, our pride, feeding our egotism, we too need to hear the words that God spoke to David through Nathan, "I anointed you; I delivered you; I gave you, (provided for your every need), and if this were not enough I would add as much again for you. Why have you shown contempt for Yahweh (me), doing what displeases him (me) (2Samuel 12: 7-9)? "You worked in secret, I will work this in the face of all Israel and the face of the sun" (2 Samuel 12:12). There is no point in trying to conceal our actions from God. David had turned his back on God, but God did not give up on him. He sent Nathan to help him admit the truth and to face up to the reality of the situation. "Everything that is now covered will be uncovered, and everything now hidden will be made clear" (Matthew 10:38).

Nathan who was a prophet at the royal court, and a successor to Samuel, not only exposed the sin of David but also prophesied that although David would live to old age bloodshed within his own family would bring calamity upon him. David then said to Nathan, "'I have sinned against Yahweh" (12:13). The denial was no more, he had confessed, admitted to God, Nathan, and himself that he had been unfaithful and had caused hurt and pain to all he professed he loved. In return, Nathan said, "Yahweh for his part, forgives your sin; you are not to die. Yet because you have outraged Yahweh by doing this, the child that is born to you is to die" (12:14-15). And just as the prophecy had foretold the child did indeed fall gravely ill. However, David's reaction to the illness showed a man filled with remorse for his actions. "He pleaded with Yahweh for the child: kept a strict fast, went home every night and slept on bare ground; covered (himself) in sacking, (a sign of true repentance) (12:16).

How different was David's reaction to all those people since that time who have given into a night of passion, a lustful urge which led to the creation of life, and whose first reaction was to get rid of that child, to abort it? One of the recent comments used to aid a change of the abortion laws in Ireland was, "It is my body, I want to have control over it." Quite ironic as it was the lack of control, of self-control that led to a child being conceived. It is the child, not the woman who has no control, no one to acknowledge its existence as a human living embryo. And just like David found, trying to cover up indiscretions, even by murder, does not dissolve the situation, indeed it all leads to greater misery and a deterioration in the physical, emotional, and spiritual life.

After the child died, David who had shown true grief, got up, bathed (cleansed himself); anointed himself (healing oil used to cover wounds and aid in their healing), and put on fresh clothes (awareness of sin). The clothes, which were often used as a metaphor in the Bible referred to the atonement of the sin, especially of that very first sin committed by Adam and Eve. "Then the eyes of both of them were opened and they realised they were naked. So they went and sewed fig leaves together to make themselves loincloths" (Genesis 3:7). Their awareness caused them to immediately attempt to rectify their condition by constructing garments from fig leaves. Just as in the story of David and Bathsheba, sin always has negative consequences and will bring hurt and pain to our fellow man and so there needs to be an atonement, the action of making amends for a wrong or injury.

In Genesis, God showed Adam and Eve how to atone for their sin. "Yahweh God made clothes out of skins for the man and his wife, and they put them on" (Genesis 3:21). An animal had to be killed or sacrificed so that its skin could be used to take away Adam and Eve's sin. Thus through sacrificial death atonement for sin was achieved. It was only after atonement

145

was made that Adam and Eve could enter into a new relationship, or covenant with God – a covenant that had been lost after the Fall and it is this new reconciled status that is depicted by their clothing. Their clothing became an ever-present reminder of the atonement that had been made on their behalf and their new covenant with God.

Just as the fall of Adam and Eve was forgiven by God so too was the fall from grace by David. And when David showed atonement, God in his loving, merciful kindness blessed David. "David consoled his wife, Bathsheba" (2 Samuel: 12–24). He offered her comfort in her time of grief. By this action, David proved that he had accepted full responsibility for his guilt. Then in a true, loving act, He went to her and slept with her" (2 Samuel 12:24). This was an act of atonement, carried out in love, which in turn produced fruit.

"She conceived and gave birth to a son whom she named Solomon" (Samuel: 13-25). This child was to grow up and become one of Israel's greatest kings, and an ancestor of Jesus. Solomon began his reign in true humility. "Now Yahweh my God, you have made your servant king in succession to David my father. But I am a very young man, unskilled in leadership…Give your servant a heart to understand how to discern between good and evil, for who can govern these people of yours so great?" (1 Kings 37–10). God was so pleased with Solomon because he had "asked for a discerning judgement for yourself…I will give you a heart wise and shrewd as none before you has had and none will have after you" (1Kings 3:12).

Solomon was credited with building the first temple in Jerusalem, which he dedicated to Yahweh, the God of Israel. He is portrayed as great in wisdom, wealth and power beyond either of the previous kings of the country, but unfortunately, like his father, David, towards the end of his reign, he too fell into sin. His sins included idolatry, marrying foreign women and, ultimately, turning away from Yahweh. No matter how clever, powerful, or even spiritual both Solomon and David were, during their reign they showed a lack of self-control, they didn't say 'no' to their selfish desires. Jesus, a descendant of David's, on the other hand, demonstrated complete self-control, throughout His time on earth. His public ministry began after He had spent forty days in the desert and had been tempted by Satan. The temptation of Christ is described in the Gospels of Matthew, Mark, and Luke. According to scripture, after being baptized by John the Baptist, and receiving the power of the Holy Spirit, Jesus fasted for 40 days and nights in the Judean Desert.

Fasting traditionally presaged a great spiritual struggle as demonstrated by Elijah, when after his fast, Elijah ran away to a high mountain and stayed there until God spoke to him in a gentle voice and revealed his future mission to him. Moses also fasted on Mount Sinai before presenting the Ten Commandments to the people. "Moses was there with the Lord forty days and forty nights without eating bread or drinking water. And he wrote on the tablets the words of the covenant – the Ten Commandments" (Exodus 34:28, NIV). Actually, the term Forty days when used in the Old Testament could refer to a complete number, not necessarily the digit representing the object. However, the fact that they fasted is important because it is a demonstration of self-control being put into practice, the denial of food and water, for oneself.

Indeed the concept of fasting is very relevant throughout the Old and New Testaments and is especially relevant and even needed in our Church's today. In the Old Testament, it was often a way of expressing grief or a means of humbling oneself before the Lord, as was displayed who humbled himself with fasting. "Yet, when they were sick, I put sackcloth on, I humbled my soul with fasting" (Psalm 35:13). In the New Testament, although there is also an element of humility e.g. Lent, fasting has and is, a means to grow closer to God, a way of being able to meditate and focus on God while denying the flesh. Indeed throughout the New Testament fasting and prayer, or communicating with God, are often mentioned together, "One day while they were offering worship to the Lord and keeping a fast, the Holy Spirit said, 'I want Barnabas and Saul set apart for the work to which I have called them. So it was that after fasting and prayer they laid hands on them and sent them off'" (Acts 13: 2–4).

In worship, fasting allows us to 'cling' to the Lord. "It is Yahweh, your God, you must fear and serve; you must cling to him; in his name take your oaths." (Deuteronomy 10:20) The word for 'cling', in the Talmud, is *devekut*. According to Chaim Bentorah, in his Biblical Hebrew Studies website, in Modern Hebrew, *devekut,* is actually used for the word, *glue.* Thus there is this metaphorical situation of us gluing ourselves to God or adhering to Him. "Rabbinic literature teaches that *Devekut* is a high and deep stage of spiritual development where the seeker attaches him or herself to God and exchanges individuality for a profound partnership with God. The force behind a *Devekut* is the love of God and desire for intimacy or closeness with God" (www.chaimbentorah.com).

Following the example of Jesus and the Early Church believers, we too can draw near to God in a deep and profound partnership, through our worship and practice of self-control. Jesus even gave us guidance on religious observance. Almsgiving, prayer and fasting were central elements in the Jewish religion and in Matthew's gospel Jesus spoke of how and why we should incorporate these elements into our religious practice. "When you fast do not put on a gloomy look as the hypocrites do: they pull long faces to let men know they are fasting. I tell you solemnly, they have had their reward. But when you fast put oil on your head and wash your face, so that no one will know you are fasting except your Father who sees all that is done in secret; and your Father who sees all that is done in secret will reward you" (Matthew 6: 16–19). Thus secret religion, or that which is done for God and not for human approval, may expect a heavenly reward. How great a reward is that to have a deep and profound relationship with the God of love?

Is it this deep relationship with the Father, and empowered with the Holy Spirit that led Jesus into the wilderness for forty days? "Then Jesus was led by the Spirit out into the wilderness to be tempted by the devil. He fasted for forty days and forty nights, after which he was very hungry and the tempter came and said to him, 'If you are the son of God, tell these stones to turn into loaves'" (Matthew 4: 1–4).

This is the first of the three recorded temptations that occurred in the desert and all the temptations are common to all mankind. The first temptation concerns the lust of the flesh, (hedonism). After the forty days fast, Jesus is hungry, and the devil tempts Him to convert stones into bread, but He replies with Scripture, quoting Deuteronomy, "Man does not live by bread alone but that man lives on every word that comes from the mouth of God" (8:3). Previously in this chapter, Moses had reminded his people, "Remember how Yahweh your God led you for forty years in the wilderness, to humble you, to test you and to know your innermost heart – whether you would keep his commandments or not. He humbled you, made you hungry, he fed you with manna which neither you nor your fathers had known, to make you understand that man does not live on bread alone" (Deuteronomy 8:2–4).

The second temptation concerns the pride of life or egoism. "The devil then took him to the Holy City and made him stand on the parapet of the temple. "'If you are the son of God,' he said, 'throw yourself down'" (Matthew 4:5–7); and here the devil uses a verse of Scripture, "for the scripture says, 'He will put you in his angels charge, And they will support you on their hands, In case you hurt your foot against a stone'"(Psalm 91:11–12).

"Jesus replied again with Scripture, 'You must not put the Lord your God to the test'" (Deuteronomy 6:16), stating that it is wrong for Him to abuse His powers and unlike David and the Israelites, He would trust in His Father's care without the need to test it by forcing God's hand.

The third temptation concerns the lust of the eyes or materialism. "Next taking him to a very high mountain, the devil showed him all the kingdoms of the world and their splendour. 'I will give you all of these' he said, 'if you fall at my feet and worship me' (Matthew 4:8–10), and if any quick route to the Messiahship could be attained, bypassing the passion and crucifixion for which He had originally come, this was the way. The devil already had control over the kingdoms of the world, 'You used to live in sin, just like the rest of the world, obeying the devil – the commander of the powers in the unseen world. He is the spirit at work in the hearts of those who refuse to obey God'" (Ephesians 2:2, NIV), but Satan was offering to relinquish this power to Jesus, in return for His allegiance. However, Jesus firmly rejected the 'shortcut' to the fulfilment of his mission which would come at a cost, that of compromising his loyalty to his father. Thus He replies sharply and again quoting scripture "You shall worship the Lord your God and serve Him only" (Deuteronomy 6:13).

Jesus, at the beginning of the next chapter in Matthew's gospel, chapter 5, starts by giving the Sermon on the Mount and finishes by speaking about temptation and self-control. "Do not imagine that I have come to abolish the Law or the Prophets. I have come not to abolish but to complete them" (5:17). "You have learnt how it was said: You must not commit adultery. But I say this to you; if a man looks at a woman lustfully, he has already committed adultery with her in his heart. If your right hand should cause you to sin, tear it out and throw it away; for it will do you less harm to lose one part of you than to have your whole body thrown into hell. And if your right hand should cause you to sin, cut it off and throw it away; for it will do you less harm to lose one part of you than to have your whole body go to hell" (Matthew 5: 27-31).

These are very strong words and are used literally to convey the seriousness of sin. Jesus is not advocating self-mutilation but rather self-denial. What he means to say is we must be sensitive to sin and renounce it and run from it and do whatever it takes to avoid it.

It is not the external act merely, which is the sin. The origin of our sin begins within us. It springs from the secrets of our hearts, from where the desire grows. That is why the psalmist cried out, "Create in me a pure heart, O God" (Psalm 51:10). As Jesus warned unless we acknowledge and act upon our desires, we will allow them to grow and fester, like a cancerous tumour. Unchecked they can grow, spread out and destroy all healthy growth, eventually causing death. The sooner the tumour is discovered, the sooner it can be removed, and consequently the less damage it will do. And so it is with our spiritual life, where the heart is not right drastic action is needed before it results in outward sin.

However, Jesus was aware of our frailness and that is why he said, "If you love me, keep my commands. And I will ask the Father, and he will give you another advocate to help you and be with you forever, the Spirit of truth whom the world cannot accept him because it neither sees him nor knows him. But you know him, for he lives with you and will be in you. I will not leave you as orphans; I will come to you. Before long, the world will not see me anymore, but you will see me. Because I live, you also will live. On that day you will realize that I am in my Father, and you are in me, and I am in you. Whoever has my commands and keeps them is the one who loves me. The one who loves me will be loved by my Father, and I too will love them and show myself to them" (John 14:15-22).

Paul also recognised his weakness, "Therefore, so that I would not become arrogant, a thorn in the flesh was given to me, a messenger of Satan to trouble me – so that I would not become arrogant. I asked the Lord three times about this, that it would depart from me. But he said to me, 'My grace is enough for you, for my power is made perfect in weakness.' So then, I will boast most gladly about my weaknesses, so that the power of Christ may reside in me. Therefore I am content with weaknesses, with insults, with troubles, with persecutions and difficulties for the sake of Christ, for whenever I am weak, then I am strong" (2 Corinthians 12: 7–11, NIV). Paul knew that Jesus had empowered him with His grace, His help, His Holy Spirit to overcome his temptations. "For the Spirit God gave us does not make us timid, but gives us power, love and self-discipline" (2 Timothy 1:7).

Finally, grow strong in the Lord with the strength of his power. Put God's armour on so that you may be able to resist the devil. For our struggle is not against flesh and blood, but against the rulers, against the powers, against the world rulers of this darkness, against the spiritual forces of evil in the heavens" (Ephesians 6:10–13). After drawing our awareness to who our real enemy is, Paul then gives us advice on how to allow the Spirit to help us fight against temptation, against Satan.

"For this reason, take up the full armour of God so that you may be able to stand your ground on the evil day, and having done everything, to stand. Stand firm, therefore, by fastening the belt of truth around your waist, by putting on the breastplate of righteousness, by fitting your feet with the preparation that comes from the good news of peace, and in all of this, by taking up the shield of faith with which you can extinguish all the flaming arrows of the evil one. And take the helmet of salvation and the sword of the Spirit, which is the word of God. With every prayer and petition, pray at all times in the Spirit, and to this end be alert, with all perseverance and requests for all the saints. Pray for me also, that I may be given the message when I begin to speak – that I may confidently make known the mystery of the gospel, for which I am an ambassador in chains. Pray that I may be able to speak boldly as I ought to speak" (Matthew 6 14-20).

Just like Paul, we need to pray this prayer every day, and then we too can, in the words of the hymn, "Be bold Be strong" and walk in faith and victory, in the knowledge that "The Lord your God is with you".

Conclusion Love

"What the Spirit brings is very different: love, joy, peace, patience, kindness, goodness faithfulness, gentleness and self-control" (Galatians 5: 22).

God is love and the very first fruit of the Spirit is love. All the other fruits, joy, peace, patience, kindness, goodness, faithfulness, self-control are bonded together in this fruit of love: Love of God, love of our neighbour; and love of ourselves. Love is the main stalk of the vine, connecting the branches, allowing nourishment to flow through so they, in turn, may produce the fruit, 'fruit which will last'. We can't produce fruit on our own and that is why God has put His Spirit within us, the Spirit of love. Fruit of the Spirit is evidence, or the proof, of the spirit of God moving through us, living within us. Love, the characteristics of God himself.

And according to Saint Paul, it doesn't matter which other fruits we may be developing within our spiritual life, if they are not carried out in love then our Christian life lacks power; it lacks victory. He went on to claim that even if we display the Gifts of the Holy Spirit in our lives, without love we become empty, we become hollow, unproductive in working for the Kingdom. "If I have all the eloquence of men or angels, but speak without love" (without gentleness, lacking patience), "I am simply a gong booming or a cymbal clashing. If I have the gift of prophecy, understanding all the mysteries there are, and knowing everything and if I have faith in all its fullness (living in faithfulness), to move mountains, but without love, then I am nothing at all" (1 Corinthians 13: 13).

Paul speaks of using the gift of prophecy, the ability to receive a divinely inspired message, which is given to some believers, by the Holy Spirit, and makes known the secrets of God's heart. The Gifts, when combined with faith, mountain-moving faith, that which produces miracles, means nothing if it is done, without love. According to Paul, not only is it worthless, but it can be damaging. The absence of love in ministry means that I am changed for the worse, 'I have become hollow, 'I am nothing' and 'I gain nothing for all my effort'. Paul, then continues in the same vein, "If I give away all I possess, (kindness, self-control) piece by piece, and if I let them take my body to burn it (peace) but am without love, it will do me no good whatever" (1 Corinthians 13:1–4). Even if generosity overflows to the point of total self-giving, it doesn't matter because if it is done without love, or for selfish motives, then it is not pleasing to God. Because without love we are functioning mechanically, acting in a way to appease God and to win favour from our fellow man. Somehow the Christian Religion, is often regarded as one which involves a set of rules, and woe betide anyone who falls foul of these. However if there is one thing we can learn from the ministry of Jesus, the Christian religion is based on love, not rules.

All of the actions of Jesus, throughout His ministry were carried out in love, right to the very end, death on the cross.

In Matthew's gospel, we learn how Jesus felt about love. When the Pharisees had heard that Jesus had silenced the Sadducees, they got together and "To disconcert him, one of them put a question, 'Master, which is the greatest commandment of the law?' This was quite a leading question as the Ten Commandments had been enlarged to quite a degree, to six hundred and thirteen to be precise and these included 'positive commandments', and 'negative commandments'. The negative commandments began with the words 'Thou shall not' and numbered three hundred and sixty-five; to coincide with the number of days in a year. In addition to these were positive which began with 'Thou shall' and in total numbered two hundred and forty-eight, also a significant number, one ascribed to the number of bones and main organs in the human body" (Babylonian Talmud, Makkot 23b–24a). All of the commandments were divided into two categories, those of 'greater and smaller' commandments. However, there was no agreement as to which belonged to which category, or which were more important. Some Jews claimed that it was the law respecting sacrifice; others, that it was respecting circumcision; while still others, that it was pertaining to washings and purifying, etc. Thus they were focusing on man-made rules, as a way of serving God, winning approval from him.

In answer to them, "Jesus focused on the two halves of the Ten Commandments, a duty to God and duty to our neighbour. In doing so His words offer a foundation for all our living and by summing up that duty as to love, it goes beyond the specific requirements of the law to the God-like attitude which is the manifestation of our beliefs through our actions. Jesus said, 'You must love the Lord your God with all your heart, with all your soul, and with all your mind. This is the first and the greatest of all the commandments. The second resembles it: You must love your neighbour as yourself" (Matthew 22: 32–39). In the first part of the answer, Jesus begins by referring to the doctrine of the unity of God "Hear, O Israel! The Lord thy God is one Lord. Love the Lord your God with all your heart and with all your soul and with all your strength" (Deuteronomy 6:4). This is known as the Shema taken from the first word 'hear' in Hebrew and modern Jews today consider the recital of the Shema both evening and morning to be one of their most sacred duties. It is what they strive for and what we too, as Christians, should strive to achieve.

This command is so easy to say, yet so incredibly difficult to do, when we come to analyse it. That's because, in the natural state of man, it is impossible. There is no greater evidence of the inability of a man to obey God's Law than this one commandment. We can't do it on our own, we need the empowering presence of the Holy Spirit in our lives, and to grow daily in His love. And Just as the man in Mark's gospel, asked God to help his unbelief, "I do have faith, help the little faith I have"(Mark 9:24), so we too should ask God to help us in areas where we don't love Him with all our heart, soul, mind, and strength. For it is by the His power, the power of the Holy Spirit working within us, that allows us to do the impossible, to love the unlovable; those who persecute us; our enemies. When we ask for His help He will hear and answer us. He will remove all our fears and allow us to pray as the Psalmist in Psalm 91 prayed:

He (you) rescue(s) you (me) from the snares

Of fowlers hoping to destroy you (me):

He (You) cover(s) you (me) with his (your) feathers
And you (I) find shelter under his (your) wings.

You (I) need not fear the terrors of night
The arrow that flies in daytime,
the plague what stalks in the dark
the scourge that wreaks havoc in broad daylight (91: 3–6)

No disaster can overtake you (me),
no plague come near your (my) home
He (You) will put you (me|) in his (your) angel' charge to
guard you (me|) wherever you (I) go.

They will support you (me|) on their hands
in case you (I) hurt your (my) foot against a stone;
you (I) will tread on savage lions and dragons.

I (You) will rescue all who cling to me (you),
I (You) protect whoever knows my (your) name,
I (You) answer everyone who invokes me (you),
I You) am (are) with them when they are in trouble;
I (You) bring them safety and honour.
I (You) give them life, long and full,
And show them how I (You) can save (Psalm 91 10-16).

The Midrash which is an ancient commentary on part of
the Hebrew scriptures, attached to the biblical text, claims that
Psalm 91 was composed by Moses, on the day he completed
the building of the Tabernacle in the desert. Moses knew first-
hand of God's love and protection and wanted all to come to

know the God he loved and served, and in this lies a lesson for us. We need to come to know God.

We cannot love someone we don't know, so getting to know God, should be our number one priority. Prayer, or talking to God just isn't enough. We need to read God's word, His scriptures and meditate on them; to listen in silence, so that God's spirit can bring His words alive and reveal the truth buried deep within. Also the closer we come to know someone the more we trust them, even to the point of sharing our deepest secrets with them; those secrets which were hidden, concealed. Trust is two ways when we reveal our secrets, then the person listening to them will also reveal themselves to us and so it is with God, when we learn to sit quietly and listen to him in the silence of our hearts, He will share his sadness; His joy, His love with us.

Our love and affection for God will grow more intense, the more time we devote to talking and listening to Him. Also, we desperately need the support of Christian fellowship. For it is through the witness of God's faithfulness during times of struggle and trial that enables a deep faith in, and love for God, which when properly nourished will grow and grow and we will begin to see the world through His eyes, and the need for the love of our neighbour because from the heart "flow the springs of life"(Proverbs 4:23), and without one's will, desires, passions, affections, perceptions, and thoughts rightly aligned, the life of love is impossible.

Paul in his letter to the Corinthians was stating quite clearly what life without love meant. He claimed that even if you are a practising Christian with some of the greatest gifts of God flowing through you, but if you are not walking in the spirit of love and humility, then you are in darkness, walking away from the light, with a deceptive heart. It is the presence of love that affirms others and overcomes destructive aspects of our character. Paul even gave us a blueprint for how we show love in our lives, "Love is always patient and kind; it is never jealous, love is never boastful or conceited; it is never rude or selfish; it does not take offence, and it is not resentful. Love takes no pleasure in other people's sins but delights in the truth (1 Corinthians 13: 4–7). In other words, aspects of love, coincide with fruits of the Spirit of; joy, peace, patience, kindness, goodness, faithfulness, gentleness, and self-control.

Thus these nine fruits which come directly from the Holy Spirit allow us to lead a life that is pleasing to God as they are grounded in love. Jesus told us that He is the vine, and we are the branches. Branches draw life from the vine, and just as the branch draws its life from the vine, so too must we draw our life directly from Jesus. Jesus will release His divine life directly into us through the Holy Spirit in the same way that the vine will release the life of the tree into the branches. And it is Jesus's Spirit living in our hearts that will bring to fruition all that is good. The fruit that is produced from all loving acts towards God and our fellow man will be stored in heaven where it will become crystallized, change into precious stones, pearls, diamonds, rubies, sapphires, emeralds. And all this can happen when we allow Jesus to reign supreme in our hearts, through His Holy Spirit. We can walk in love and joy for the 'King is in residence there'. (Hymn Joy Is the Flag. Writer unknown.)

1859